BEADWORK

Creates

D1635306

Necklaces

edited by **Jean Campbell**

 INTERWEAVE PRESS

Text and illustrations copyright © 2002 Interweave Press, Inc.

Photography copyright © 2002 Joe Coca and Interweave Press Inc.

Interweave Press
201 East Fourth Street
Loveland, Colorado 80537 USA
www.interweave.com

Printed and bound in China through Asia Pacific Offset

Library of Congress Cataloging-in-Publication Data

Campbell, Jean, 1964-
  Beadwork creates necklaces / Jean Campbell.
      p. cm.
Includes bibliographical references and index.
  ISBN 1-931499-22-5
  1. Beadwork—Patterns. 2. Necklaces. I. Beadwork (Loveland, Colo.) II.
Title.
  TT860 .C3574 2002
  745.58'2--dc21

                                2002006956

10 9 8 7 6 5 4 3

Project editor: Jean Campbell
Technical editor: Dustin Wedekind
Illustrations: Ann Swanson
Photography: Joe Coca
Book design and production: Paulette Livers
Proofreader: Nancy Arndt

Dear Reader,

A beautiful necklace accents the face like a fine frame. It is a piece of jewelry that can make a bold statement or provide just a hint of accessory. It is the first thing you look at when you meet another beadworker, and touching each other's necklaces has wittily become known as the "beadworkers' handshake."

As editor of *Beadwork*® magazine, I have great beadwork designs cross my desk every day. *Beadwork Creates Necklaces* is a collection of thirty of my favorite necklace projects—all original pieces designed by leaders in the field. The projects feature stringing, peyote and herringbone stitch, netting, crochet, and wirework, and they range from easy to advanced in technique.

I've included a Tips section at the back of the book (page 106) that you should be sure to read; it will help you as you start each project. There is also a Stitches section (page 107) that clearly defines each stitch used in the book; it's a handy tool for those who need to learn new stitches or are just feeling a little rusty.

Now pick your favorite necklace, take this book to your local bead shop, make your purchases, and get beading—you've got a masterpiece to create!

—Jean Campbell
Editor, *Beadwork*
magazine and books

Con

On the cover, Vesselage, p. 25
Title page, Crochet Braid, p. 18

tents

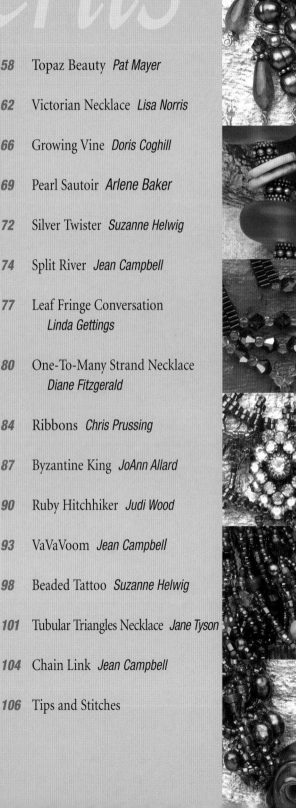

Resinate

Judy Tomsky

Materials
20 olivine 19mm resin rondelles
38 African ostrich shell disks
Forty-eight 5mm Bali silver spacers
Four 2mm crimp beads
One 2⅛" silver clasp
24" of Soft Flex .019" beading wire

Notions
Wire cutter
Crimping pliers

This striking green and silver necklace is simple to make and easy to wear.

Step 1: String 2 crimp beads and pass the end of the wire through one side of the clasp. Pass back through the crimp beads leaving a 2" tail. Snug the crimp beads close to the clasp and crimp the beads.

Step 2: String 5 spacers and 1 rondelle, making sure to cover the tail with the beads. *String 1 spacer, 2 ostrich disks, 1 spacer, 1 rondelle. Repeat from * 18 times. String 5 spacers.

Step 3: String 2 crimp beads and pass the end of the wire through the other side of the clasp. Pass back through the crimp beads and as many beads on the wire as possible. Snug up all the beads to let out any slack. Crimp the beads.

Judy Tomsky is the sole proprietor of Natural Touch beads. She works with bead makers in Indonesia to produce cottage-made industry beads for her wholesale business in Sonoma, California, and for her own designs. Judy's wares can be seen at trade shows around the country or through her website www.naturaltouchbeads.com; ntbeads@aol.com; PO Box 351, Sonoma, CA 95476; (707) 935-7049.

Retro Filigree

Arlene Baker

Materials

41 round 6mm glass beads
1 glass 8 x 12mm drop to match beads
1 glass 18mm x 13mm cabochon to match beads
1 brass filigree triangle (#842)
1 brass filigree flourish (#839)
1 brass 18 x 13 setting (#870)
1 brass ½" x ⁹⁄₁₆" oval disk (#749)
1 brass 7mm cap (#620)
39 oval brass jump rings (#20/25)
3 oval brass jump rings (#35/28)
Two head pins 1½" long
Forty eye pins 1½" long
Brass hook
Epoxy or E6000

Notions

Wire cutter
Smooth-jaw needle-nose pliers
Round-nose pliers
Heavy-duty cutter
Metal file (rasp)
Toothpicks

This beautiful old-style necklace employs beaded chain and a pendant made from reconstructed filigree that is designed just for the centerpiece. The filigree used in this necklace is from Eastern Findings Corporation, (800) EFC-6640, www.efcsales@easternfindings.com.

Step 1: Use the heavy-duty cutter to cut the filigree flourish in half at the delicate leaves between the heart-like shapes. File the rough edges smooth with the metal file.

Step 2: Wash all the brass pieces in hot soapy water and dry thoroughly.

Step 3: Use a toothpick to apply a thin coat of glue on the back of the flourish. Place the flourish on top of the right side of the triangle and press the two pieces together. The widest part of the flourish should sit near the widest part of the triangle. Let glue dry.

Step 4: Apply a thin coat of glue on the back of the setting. Place the setting on top of the portion of the pendant made in Step 3 and center it. Press it down firmly and let glue dry.

Step 5: Apply a thin coat of glue on the back of the disk. Glue the disk to the back of the triangle to hide any glue that has oozed through the filigree. Press it in place so it lines up evenly with the setting. Let glue dry.

Step 6: Apply a thin coat of glue to the back of the cabochon and press it into the setting. Let glue dry.

Step 7: *Use an eye pin to string one 6mm. Snug the bead to the loop and cut the wire on the other side about ½" from the bead. Use the tip of your round-nose pliers to make a loop on this side. Make both loops face the same direction. Repeat from * 39 times.

Step 8: Use a head pin to string one 6mm. Cut the wire ½" from the bead and make a loop.

Step 9: Use a head pin to string the drop and a bead cap. Cut the wire ½" from the bead cap and make a loop.

Step 10: Attach a 35/28 jump ring to the upper left corner of the brass triangle. Open one loop of a looped bead and attach it to the jump ring. Close the loop. Open the other loop on the looped bead and attach a 20/25 jump ring. Close the loop. *Open a loop on another looped bead. Attach it to the jump ring just added. Close the loop. Open the other loop on the looped bead and attach a 20/25 jump ring. Close the loop. Repeat from * 15 times. Attach the hook to the jump ring.

Step 11: Attach a 35/28 jump ring to the upper right corner of the brass triangle. Open one loop of a looped bead and attach it to the jump ring. Close the loop. Open the other loop on the looped bead and attach a 20/25 jump ring. Close the loop. *Open a loop on another looped bead. Attach it to the jump ring just added. Close the loop. Open the other loop on the looped bead and attach a 20/25 jump ring. Close the loop. Repeat from * 21 times. Attach the head pin bead to the jump ring.

Step 12: Attach a 35/28 jump ring to the bottom corner of the brass triangle. Attach a beaded loop to the jump ring. Attach the drop bead to the beaded loop.

Arlene Baker is a frequent contributor to Beadwork. *She is the author of* Beads in Bloom, *published by Interweave Press. Arlene can be reached at (562) 928-3583.*

Double Happiness

Deb Dzuris

Materials.
1 strand 2.5mm round pink coral beads
1 strand 2.5mm round turquoise beads
2 medium sterling silver cones
Sterling silver hook and eye clasp
2 sterling silver eye pins
1 sterling silver 8mm jump ring
1 earring
17" of Soft Touch .010" beading wire
2 silver crimp beads

Notions
Wire cutter
Crimping pliers
Round-nose pliers

The first Happiness of this necklace is you get to use that earring you've been holding on to. The second Happiness is all the compliments you'll receive!

Step 1: Use the wire to string one crimp bead. Pass through an eye pin and back through the crimp bead leaving a 1" tail. Snug the bead close to the eye pin and crimp the bead.

Step 2: String 15" of coral beads and 1 crimp bead. Pass through the other eye pin, back through the crimp bead, and through as many of the coral beads as possible. Snug up all to get rid of any slack. Squeeze the crimp bead and trim the wire close to the work.

Step 3: Repeat Steps 1 and 2 for the turquoise beads, using the same two eye pins.

Step 4: Pull one of the eye pins (straight wire side) through one of the cones (Figure 1). Make a hangman's noose loop on that side of the cone, incorporating one side of the clasp and pulling tight to relieve any slack. Repeat for the other end of the strand.

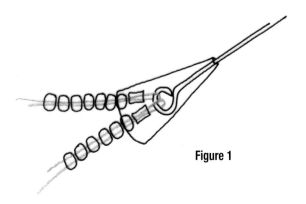

Figure 1

Step 5: Open a jump ring and attach the earring. Thread both strands through the jump ring. Close the jump ring.

Deb Dzuris is the proprietor of 4th Street Bead, 118 East 4th Street, Loveland, CO 80537.

The Moon is Made of Brie Cheese

Betcey Ventrella

Materials

20mm carved stone cabochon
Size 15° seed beads in pearl, shiny white,
    and gold
21 bicone 3mm clear crystals
35 bicone 4mm clear crystals
13 bicone 6mm clear crystals
24 round gold 4mm fire-polished beads
11 clear 8mm daggers
2" x 2" piece of Lacy's Stiff Stuff
2-part epoxy
Size B or D white or ivory beading thread
1 yard of Soft Touch .010" beading wire
Leather (deerskin or ultrasuede)
Aileen's Leather Glue

Notions

Size 12 beading needle
Scissors
Wire cutters
Pen
Crimping or needle-nose pliers

This dreamy necklace is a delightful way to use cabochons.
The piece was named in response to a dream the designer had.
She insisted this creamy cabochon go in the refrigerator every
fifteen minutes so it wouldn't get runny!

BEADING THE CABOCHON

Step 1: Glue your cabochon into place on the Stiff Stuff. Be
sure that the glue gets evenly spread to the edges of the cabochon so your bead embroidery can sit tightly against it. Allow
the cabochon to sit overnight before proceeding.

Step 2: Using a yard of thread with a knot at the end, pass through the Stiff Stuff from back to front near the edge of the cabochon.

Round 1: Use white beads to make a backstitched ring around the cabochon. Hug the curve of the cabochon and keep it as snug as you can. The round of beads should be tight enough so there isn't any thread showing. Adjust the counts slightly toward the end of the round for a snug fit. When you've finished the round, pass your needle to the right side of the Stiff Stuff about a half-bead's width away from this round.

Round 2: Continue backstitching 3 beads at a time, following the lines of Round 1, but alternate with white and gold.

Round 3: Use pearl beads to repeat Round 1. Make a knot on the back side of the work and trim.

Step 3: Trim the Stiff Stuff so that none shows around the beadwork. Don't snip too closely, you might cut the threads.

STRAP

Figure 1

Step 4: Center the Soft Touch around the back side of the cabochon. Starting at the bottom, use a needle and thread to sew the Soft Flex around the edge of the cab in a U shape (Figure 1). Take extra care not to let the stitches show on the front side of your beadwork. Make small stitches.

ATTACHING THE LEATHER

Step 5: Put the beaded cabochon on top of the leather piece and use a pen to trace around the cabochon on the suede/rough side of the leather. Cut the outline, following ever so slightly on the inside of the line.

Step 6: Smear a thin layer of glue and press lightly. Allow to dry for at least 15 minutes.

Step 7: Use white beads and a simple picot edging (Figure 2) to attach the beaded piece to the leather backing.

Figure 2

STRAP

Step 8: String 3 pearl, one 6mm, 1 pearl, one 4mm fire-polished, 1 pearl, one 4mm crystal, 1 pearl, one 3mm crystal, 1 pearl, 3 gold, 40 pearl, and 3 gold.

Step 9: Repeat Step 8 twice so you have three total sections of crystals. Adjust the amount of seed beads in the last segment to make the length of your necklace suitable.

Step 10: String a crimp tube and one side of the clasp. Pass back through the crimp tube and several of the beads strung in Step 9. Pull tight to take up any slack and crimp the tube.

Step 11: Repeat Steps 8–10 for the other side.

FRINGE

Step 12: Pass the needle under the leather backing and tie a knot around an edge stitch to secure. Exit from the sixth picot bead from the bottom-center bead of the edging.

Leg 1: 10 pearl, one 3mm crystal, 1 pearl, one 4mm crystal, 1 pearl, one 4mm fire-polished, 1 pearl, 2 gold, 1 dagger, and 2 gold. Skipping the last three beads, pass back through all the rest of the beads and pass through the next picot to position for the next leg.

Leg 2: 12 pearl, one 3mm crystal, 1 pearl, one 4mm crystal, 1 pearl, one 4mm fire-polished, 1 pearl, one 4mm crystal, 1 pearl, 2 gold, 1 dagger, and 2 gold.

Leg 3: 14 pearl, one 3mm crystal, 1 pearl, one 4mm crystal, 1 pearl, one 4mm fire-polished, 1 pearl, one 4mm crystal, 1 pearl, one 6mm crystal, 1 pearl, 2 gold, 1 dagger, and 2 gold.

Leg 4: 3 white, 14 pearl, one 3mm crystal, 1 pearl, one 4mm crystal, 1 pearl, one 4mm fire-polished, 1 pearl, one 4mm crystal, 1 pearl, one 6mm crystal, 1 pearl, one 4mm crystal, 1 pearl, 2 gold, 1 dagger, and 2 gold.

Leg 5: 5 white, 14 pearl, one 3mm crystal, 1 pearl, one 4mm crystal, 1 pearl, one 4mm fire-polished, 1 pearl, one 4mm crystal, 1 pearl, one 6mm crystal, 1 pearl, one 4mm crystal, 1 pearl, one 4mm fire-polished, 1 pearl, 2 gold, 1 dagger, and 2 gold.

Leg 6: 7 white, 14 pearl, one 3mm crystal, 1 pearl, one 4mm crystal, 1 pearl, one 4mm fire-polished, 1 pearl, one 4mm crystal, 1 pearl, one 6mm crystal, 1 pearl, one 4mm crystal, 1 pearl, one 4mm fire-polished, 1 pearl, one 3mm crystal, 1 pearl, 2 gold, 1 dagger, and 2 gold.

Legs 7–11: Repeat Legs 5–1.

Betcey Ventrella is the all-knowing goddess of Beyond Beadery in Rollinsville, Colorado. Contact her at (303) 258-9389; betcey@beyondbeadery.com; www.beyondbeadery.com.

Crochet Braid

Doris Coghill

Materials

Pearls, stone chips, drops or other accent beads
40–60 yards of 28-gauge wire
6" of 20-gauge wire
Clasp
2 cones or barrel caps
2 split rings

Notions

Size G or larger crochet hook
Round-nose pliers
Needle-nose pliers
Wire cutter

You don't need to know how to crochet to make this light and fanciful piece.

Step 1: Without cutting the wire from the spool, string the beads on the wire. Your bead quantity will depend on how thick you want the finished piece to be.

Step 2: Form a slipknot with the wire. Insert the crochet hook through the loop, leaving a loop of about ½". Catch the wire with the crochet hook and pull it back through the loop. The hook should be under the wire. Turn the tip of the hook to the left, catching the wire. Continue turning the hook down and towards you, pulling it back through the loop (Figure 1). This is called a chain stitch.

Step 3: Push a bead up so that it touches the completed loop, and then do another chain stitch. Continue alternating plain chain stitches and pushing up beads until the strand is the desired length for your necklace.

Finish the strand with a chain stitch. Remove the hook, leaving the loop, and cut the wire about 5" from the stitches. Complete nine of these strands all the same length. Gently stretch each strand after completing it.

Figure 1

Step 4: *Three Braid method:* Gather three of the strands at the end where you started to crochet. Lightly twist the three strands of wire together directly above the first chain stitch. Braid the three strands together. If the rows are not the same length, adjust by adding or removing stitches and/or beads before you finish the braiding. Repeat twice more, ending up with three braided pieces of the same length. Lightly twist these three pieces together directly above the first stitch and braid the three braids together. Do not twist the braids together so densely that they won't fit into your cone ends.

Single Braid method: Align all nine strands at the end where you started to crochet. Lightly twist the strands together directly above the first chain stitch. Separate the strands into three groups and braid these groups. If the strands are not the same length, adjust by adding or removing stitches and/or beads before you finish the braiding.

Using 3" of the 20-gauge wire, bend a J-shape about ½" from the end of the wire. Insert the J-shape into where you twisted the strands together then wrap the twisted wire ends of the crocheted strands around the J-shape several times, being sure it is secure. Squeeze the J-shape to secure the twisted ends and wrap the short end of the wire up the wire (Figure 2). Continue wrapping the remaining wire crocheted ends around the J-shape, but test to be sure it will still fit inside the cone pieces you are planning to finish the end with. Cut off excess wire.

Slide the cone onto the long part of the J-shape wire as far into the end piece as possible, being sure all wire ends are inside. Use a round-nose pliers to make a loop with the remaining part of the J-shape about ½" above the top of the cone. Wrap the end of the wire back around itself (between the loop and the cone) to secure. Cut off any excess wire. Attach a split ring and clasp to the loop.

Figure 2

Doris Coghill has been working with seed beads for about nine years, but has been involved with some type of crafts all her life. She is currently busy with designing and teaching beadwork and working with her business, Dee's Place. She can be reached at www.beadsbydee.com.

Copper and Violet

Sylvia Sur

Materials

20mm carved round amethyst bead
28mm carved flat jade ornament
20 x 12mm Swarovski topaz AB crystal drop
1 oz. size 11° beads or copper hex metallic beads (C)
1 oz. size 8° matte silver-lined Czech beads (8)
5 gr. pale violet Delicas (DB695)
Size B beading thread
One 33-yard spool of Gutermann Top Stitching
and Buttonhole polyester thread
2 brass bead caps
3 brass eye pins
1 brass head pin
1 large brass jump ring
2 small brass jump rings
Brass clasp

Notions

Wire or Big Eye needle
Size 12 beading needle
Size 12 or 13 steel crochet hook
Scissors

The carved amethyst and jade beads that adorn this necklace were inspiration for the rest. Any bead, cabochon with a bezel, or lampworked bead would work just as well as the amethyst. Change the color scheme to fit your focal bead.

Thanks to Pat Iverson and Martha Forsyth for their Crossing Lines crochet rope pattern.

CROCHET ROPE

Step 1: Using a wire or needle, string beads on the crochet thread until you have at least 72" of beads. Remember that the first bead you string on the spool will be the last bead you crochet.

Read the stringing sequence either right to left starting at the top (the opposite direction we usually read), or left to right starting at the bottom. Pick one direction and be consistent or the pattern will not work: 8CCCCC, 88CCCC, 8C8CCC, 8CC8CC, 8CCC8C, 8CCCC8, 8CCCCC.

Step 2: Make a slip stitch leaving a 6" tail. Chain 6 and include one bead in each chain (Figure 1). Join into a circle by inserting hook to the left side of the first bead you crocheted. Push the bead over to the right side of the hook by passing it over the hook. Slip down the next bead on the thread and pull through both loops to make a slip stitch.

Insert the hook into the left side of the next bead. Push the bead over the hook to the right side and slip down another bead. Slip stitch through both loops.

Continue working one bead into each loop in a circle until you make the length you need.

Step 3: When you are ½" to ⅜" away from finishing the tube, use the tapestry needle to sew the eye part of an eye pin to the inside of the tube. Don't worry if it's not centered; it won't show later.

Continue to bead crochet until finished. String a bead cap on the eye pin and create a hangman's noose loop to cinch up the slack. Trim off excess wire (Figure 2). Add a small jump ring to the loop. Attach one end of the clasp.

Repeat this step for the other end of the tube.

PEYOTE BAIL

Step 4: This bail was designed to fit this ornament. Adjust accordingly for yours. Using a yard of thread, string 12 Delicas. Work flat even peyote stitch for 36 rows. Join into a tube by zipping together the up beads on each side.

Figure 1

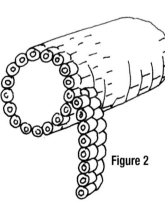

Figure 2

SQUARE-STITCHED STRIPS

Step 5: Using a yard of thread, string one tension bead and 2 Delicas. Work 13 rows of square stitch over the two Delicas, or enough rows to go through your focal ornament.

Repeat this step to create another square-stitched strip.

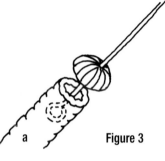

Step 6: Attach one end of one strip to the peyote tube at one side (Figure 3). Thread the focal ornament with the square-stitched strips. Leaving at least 8 rows (4 beads as you view from the side) between the two square-stitched strips, attach the second end of the strips to the peyote tube.

Figure 3

a

PENDANT

Step 7: Use the head pin to string the Swarovski drop. Measure ½" from the top of the drop and cut the pin with a wire cutters. Make a loop. Open and place an eye pin in the loop and close the eye pin. String a size 8° bead, the amethyst bead, and a size 8° bead on the eye pin. Measure ½" and cut the eye pin. Make a loop. Attach a jump ring to the bottom of the focal ornament. Attach the pendant to the focal ornament.

b

Sylvia Sur has been beading since 1994 when she discovered The New Beadwork *by Moss and Scherer. She lives in Los Angeles with husband Ed Kenney. Contact Sylvia through http://home.att.net/~ssur/ or http://home.att.net/~beadannex/.*

Vesselage

Anna Karena Tollin

Materials

Lampworked vessel
Size 6°, 8°, 11°, and 15° seed beads in a palette
    of colors to complement the vessel
Pearl, semi-precious stone, glass, and silver beads
Size B beading thread
Two-looped silver clasp
Crimp tubes
Soft Flex .014" beading wire

Notions

Size 12 beading or sharps needles
Scissors
Wire cutter

Inspired by the focal vessel made by Minneapolis lampworker Annemarie Herrlich, this free-form necklace evolved on its own. When making yours, do away with preplanning and let the beads speak to you.

PEYOTE SIDE

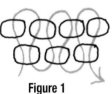

Figure 1

Step 1: Begin by working a two-bead wide peyote strap (Figure 1). Work the strap long enough to fit around the vessel handle and sew it into a circle.

Step 2: Begin to increase your stitches and start the free-form work. Anything is fair game when you're working free-form. You can make increases by adding extra beads mid-fabric (Figure 2) or you can gently change the shape and feeling of your fabric by changing the shape and size of beads used.

Figure 2

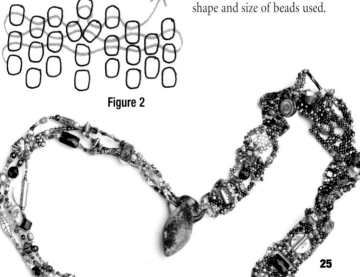

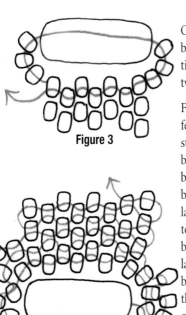

Figure 3

Figure 4

One component in free-form beadwork is the incorporation of larger beads. Here are two ways to do it.

For a horizontal hole, string a few beads off your peyote-stitched row. String the larger bead and a few beads. Pass back through the work to the beads strung right before the larger bead (Figure 3). Begin to work peyote off these beads. When you reach the larger bead, string enough beads to pass over the top of the larger bead. Work peyote on the beads strung on the other side of the larger bead. Continue working peyote back and forth above the bead (Figure 4).

For a vertical hole, decide where you'd like your bead to go and string a seed bead, the larger bead, and a seed bead. Pass back through the larger bead and the seed bead, then peyote stitch to the end of the row. *Work a thin strip of peyote until it is tall enough to reach the seed bead at the top of the larger bead. String enough beads to reach the top of the larger bead. Pass back through the larger bead and to the other side of the peyote row. Repeat from * for the other side of the row. Continue working peyote as usual all across the row (Figure 5).

Step 3: Work the peyote side of the necklace until you reach half the desired length. Be conscious that the end of this peyote section will hang in the middle of the back of

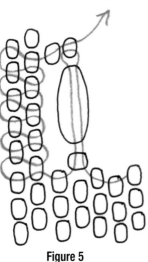

Figure 5

your neck, so make adjustments to width accordingly. Also keep in mind that the end of this section must cleanly attach to the clasp.

Step 4: Attach the beadwork to the clasp by using size 15's to work two straps of 2-bead-wide peyote that match up with the loops on the clasp. When they are long enough to reach through and wrap around the loops, weave the straps through the loops and sew back into the beadwork. Pass the thread through the beads on the body of the necklace, tie a knot between the beads, pass through several more beads to hide the knot, and trim close to work.

STRUNG SIDE

Step 5: Measure the length of the first side of your necklace. Add 3" and use a wire cutter to cut that measurement of wire. String 1 crimp tube and pass the wire through one loop and back through the crimp tube leaving a 1½" tail. Snug the tube up to the loop and crimp it.

Step 6: String an assortment of beads, making sure you cover the double tail at the beginning of the wire. While stringing, pay attention to the placement of your larger beads. Don't place them directly across from their counterparts in the peyote side. Create a few surprises by making sure that each side has a few beads the other side does not.

Step 7: When you reach about 1½" from the end, string a crimp tube and 1¼" of seed beads. Pass through the other arm of the vessel and then back through the crimp tube you just strung. Continue to pass back through as many beads as possible on the strand. Pull the wire tight, taking up any slack. Crimp the tube. Trim the tail close to the work.

Step 8: Repeat Steps 5–7 two times.

Anna Karena Tollin lives in Minneapolis, Minnesota, and was introduced to beading by her sister-in-law. Anna enjoys the problem-solving aspect of freeform beadwork and is intrigued by sculptural pieces. Contact her by e-mail at annatollin@cs.com.

Labradorite Symphony

Judi Mullins

Materials

35 bicone 4mm green vitral Swarovski crystals
5 bicone 6mm green vitral Swarovski crystals
4 labradorite 4mm round beads
90 labradorite 5mm rondelles
7 labradorite 12mm tear drops
4 labradorite 12mm cylinder beads
1 labradorite 52mm bezelled pendant with bail
86 green/gray 7mm freshwater pearls
42 round 3mm silver beads
4 round 4mm silver beads
62 Bali silver 3mm heshi
2 Bali silver studded 5mm beads
2 Bali silver 5mm rings
2 Bali silver 6mm rondelles
4 bicone Bali silver wireworked 6mm beads
2 bicone 9mm Bali silver beads
2 two-holed spacer bars
7 silver 4mm split rings
4 silver bead caps
8 silver crimp beads
2 silver lobster clasps
3' of 20-gauge silver wire
33" of Soft Flex .019" beading wire

Notions

Wire cutter
Round-nose pliers
Hemostats or clamps
Crimping pliers

Oohs and aahs are what
you'll get when this pair
of necklaces hangs
around your neck.

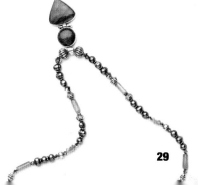

Step 1: Make the dangles by first stringing the beads on the silver wire, creating a hangman's noose loop, snugging the beads close to the loop, and making a hangman's noose loop on the other side of the beads. Attach a split ring to the top loop. Follow below for stringing instructions.

Dangles 1 and 7: Teardrop, 3mm silver.
Dangles 2 and 6: Teardrop, heishi, 3mm crystal.
Dangles 3 and 5: Bead cap, teardrop, heishi, 3mm silver, heishi, 3mm crystal.
Dangle 4: Bead cap, teardrop, bead cap, 3mm silver, 6mm crystal, 3mm silver, 3mm crystal, 3mm silver.

Step 2: Cut 15" of Soft Flex. Cut another length 18". String the beads as listed beginning with the shorter length of wire. Use hemostats or clamps to hold the wire at one end so the beads don't slide off. When finished stringing, adjust the fit by adding or removing beads at each end. The necklace should lay flat and follow the curve of your neck nicely. The smaller strand should be choker-length on your neck.

Double necklace, short strand: One 3mm crystal, *1 pearl, 1 lab rondelle, 1 heishi, 1 lab rodelle. Repeat from * twice. One pearl, one side of the spacer bar, *one 3mm crystal, 1 pearl, 1 lab rondelle, 1 heishi, 1 lab rondelle, 1 pearl, 1 lab rondelle, 1 heishi, 1 lab rondelle, 1 pearl, 1 lab rondelle, 1 heishi, 1 lab rondelle, 1 pearl. Repeat from * four times. One 3mm crystal, one side of the spacer bar, *1 pearl, 1 lab rondelle, 1 heishi, 1 lab rondelle. Repeat from * twice. One pearl, one 3mm crystal.

Double necklace, long strand: 2 lab rondelles, one 3mm crystal, 2 lab rondelles, one 3mm silver, 1 pearl, 1 heishi, 1 pearl, one 3mm silver, 2 lab rondelles, one 3mm crystal, 2 lab rondelles, the other side of the spacer bar, *one 3mm silver, 1 pearl, 1 heishi, 1 pearl, one 3mm silver round, 2 lab rondelles, one 3mm crystal, and 2 lab rondelles. Repeat from * once. String one 3mm silver, 1 pearl, 1 heishi, 1 pearl, one 3mm silver, Dangle #1, one 3mm silver. 1 pearl, 1 heishi, 1 pearl, one 3mm silver, Dangle #2, one 3mm silver. 1 pearl, 1 heishi, 1 pearl, one 3mm silver, Dangle #3, one 3mm silver. 1 pearl, 1 heishi, 1 pearl, one 3mm silver, Dangle #4, one 3mm silver. 1 pearl, 1 heishi, 1 pearl, one 3mm silver, Dangle #5, one 3mm silver. 1 pearl, 1 heishi, 1 pearl, one 3mm silver, Dangle #6, one 3mm silver. 1 pearl, 1 heishi, 1 pearl, one 3mm silver, Dangle #7, one 3mm silver. *1 pearl, 1 heishi, 1 pearl, one 3mm silver,

2 lab rondelles, one 3mm crystal, 2 lab rondelles, one 3mm silver. Repeat from * one time. 1 pearl, 1 heishi, 1 pearl, the other side of the spacer bar, 2 lab rondelles, one 3mm crystal, 2 lab rondelles, one 3mm silver, 1 pearl, 1 heishi, 1 pearl, one 3mm silver, 2 lab rondelles, one 3mm crystal, and 2 lab rondelles.

Single necklace: One 3mm crystal, 1 lab round, 4 lab rondelles, one 3mm silver, 1 pearl, 1 heishi, 1 pearl, 1 heishi, 1 pearl, one 3mm crystal, 1 lab round, one 3mm silver, 1 Bali studded, one 3mm round, one 3mm crystal, 1 pearl, 1 heishi, 1 pearl, 1 heishi, 1 pearl, one 4mm silver, 1 silver ring, one 4mm silver, one 3mm crystal, 1 lab cylinder, one 3mm crystal, 1 pearl, 1 heishi, 1 pearl, 1 heishi, 1 pearl, one 3mm crystal, 1 silver rondelle, one 3mm crystal, 3 lab rondelles, one 3mm crystal, 1 pearl, 1 heishi, 1 pearl, 1 heishi, 1 pearl, 1 silver wireworked, 1 lab cylinder, 1 silver wireworked, one 6mm crystal, 1 pearl, 1 heishi, 1 pearl, 1 heishi, 1 pearl, one 6mm crystal, 1 silver bicone, and one 3mm silver. String the pendant and work the other side of the necklace in reverse order.

Step 3: Adjust for fit by adding or subtracting beads at the beginning of each necklace. Take the short and long wire ends at one side of the necklace and string two crimp beads. Pass through one side of the clasp and back through the crimp beads leaving a 1½" tail. Snug the crimp beads close to the clasp, but not so close as to make the necklace stiff. Squeeze the beads tight with the crimping pliers.

Judi Mullins has been doing beadwork off and on for most of her adult life. She has been published in several magazines and has taught around the Northwest area. She is now teaching classes and doing beadwork designs out of her home in Tigard, Oregon. You can contact her at bead.garden@verizon.net.

Trinket Chain

Jean Campbell

Materials
Assorted beads and charms
26" heavy silver chain
4" of 20-gauge silver wire
Silver head pins
Silver jump rings or silver lobster clasps

Notions
Wire cutter
Round-nose pliers

Collect special beads, charms, and lockets to create this special necklace that shows off your wares. It will bring compliments wherever you go.

Step 1: Make a hangman's noose with the silver wire and incorporate one end of the silver chain into the loop. String a feature bead. Make a hangman's noose with the other end of the wire and incorporate the other end of the silver chain (Figure 1). Trim any excess.

Step 2: Make pendants of your beads and charms for the chain. Do this by using a head pin to string a bead or charm and finishing with a hangman's noose.

Step 3: Attach the pendants to the silver chain with jump rings or lobster clasps.

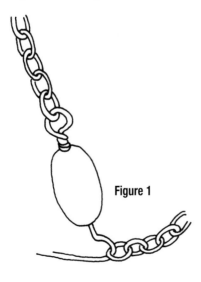

Figure 1

Tri-Star Necklace

S. Raven Willey

Materials

Fourteen 5 x 7 faceted clear AB fire-polished beads
12 black 3mm round faceted fire-polished beads
Size 8° Japanese seed beads
Size 11° Japanese seed beads in cranberry (A),
    silver-lined AB (B), and black (C)
Size 14° Japanese clear AB seed beads
Size D black Nymo beading thread
Clasp

Notions

2 size 12 beading needles
Beeswax or other conditioner
Scissors

This sumptuous necklace will make you feel like a Czarina.

PENDANTS

Make three.

Step 1: Using a yard of thread and leaving an 8" tail, string 4 size 8°s. Pass back through all four beads to form a circle. Tie a knot.

Step 2: *String 2 A, one 5 x 7, 1 A. Pass back through the 5 x 7 and the second A just strung. String 1 A and pass through the next size 8° of the base circle. Repeat from * so you add a total of four picots.

Step 3: *Pass through the first and last A strung in the next picot. String 1 B. Repeat from * all around for a total of 4 B (Figure 1). Exit from the first A strung in the first picot.

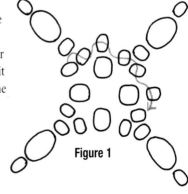

Figure 1

Step 4: Pass through the second A, the 5 x 7, and the top A of the picot. *String 6 B, then pass through the B bead that was added in the last step. String 6 B and pass through the top A of the next picot (Figure 2). Repeat from * three more times. Finish by exiting the top A of the first picot.

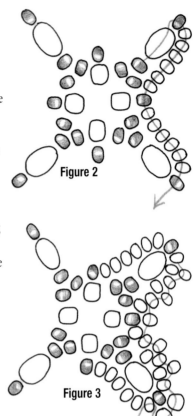

Figure 2

Step 5: *Pass through the first B of the next 6-bead strand. Make two peyote stitches using B beads. For the third stitch, string 1 B and pass through the second strung B of the next 6-bead strand. Make two more peyote stitches using B. Make the next stitch by stringing 2 size 8's and passing through the first B of the next 6-bead strand (Figure 3). Repeat this sequence from * three more times to make the first row of peyote stitch.

Figure 3

Step 6: Make a second row of peyote stitch alternating two-drop and one-drop techniques. For the *first stitch use 2 C, for the second stitch use one 3 mm, for the third stitch use 2 C, for the fourth stitch use 1 C, for the fifth stitch work 1 size 8° between the size 8's from the previous round, for the sixth stitch use 1 C. Repeat from * four times to complete the final row of the pendant. Weave the remaining thread back into the piece to secure and trim close to work.

Step 7: Thread a needle onto the tail and *string 1 size 14°. Pass through the next size 8° of the base circle. Repeat from * to add four beads. Weave the thread back into the piece to secure and trim close to work.

NECK STRAP
Step 8: Thread a needle onto each end of 70" of thread. Use the right needle to string 3 size 8's and 1 B. Pass the left needle back through the B. Take out any slack and position the beads so that there is an equal amount of thread for each needle.

Step 9: Use the right needle to string 1 B and 3 size 8°s. Pass back through the B just strung. Repeat with the left needle.

Step 10: String 1 B with the right needle. Pass the left needle through the B just strung. String 2 size 8°s with the right needle and 1 size 8° with the left needle. Pass the left needle through the second size 8° just strung.

Step 11: Use the right needle to string 1 A and 1 size 8°. Use the left needle to string 1 A. Pass the left needle through the size 8° in the opposite direction of the right needle. Use the right needle to string 1 size 8° and 1 B. Use the left needle to string 1 size 8°. Pass the left needle through the B just strung (Figure 4).

Repeat Steps 9–11 until you've reached the desired length for half your necklace strap. Note: Three full diamonds equals approximately 1½" in length after they've been firmed up. Add one half of the clasp. Weave the thread back through the piece, knot to secure, then trim close to work.

Step 12: Firm up the diamonds by threading a needle onto each end of 30" of conditioned thread and, starting at the clasp end, weaving back

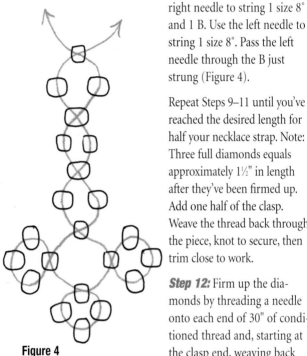

Figure 4

through the outside beads of the strap. Weave down each side and leave the remaining thread to attach a pendant.

LINKING SECTIONS

There are two of these sections. These sections contain two full diamonds each and use about 24" of thread per section. Making the sections, firming them up, and adding the oval edges are done all with the same thread.

Step 13: After firming up the diamonds on each side, position the strap so the thread end is to the right. Use the top needle to weave back up the diamond to the top size 8° bead. String 1 B, 1 A, one 5 x 7, 1 A, and 1 B. Pass through the top size 8°

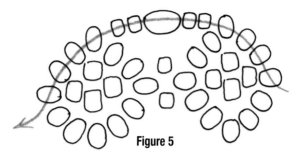

Figure 5

bead of the second diamond. Weave thread down the left side of the second diamond. Leave the tail; it will be used to attach the strap to the pendants (Figure 5).

ATTACHING THE PENDANTS

Step 14: Position the strap to the left and a pendant to the right. Make sure that all the pendants are lying with the side that shows the center size 14s facing up. Use the bottom needle of the strap to string 1 size 8°. Pass through the size 11° indicated in Figure 6. String 1 size 8° and pass through the top size 8° of the pendant.

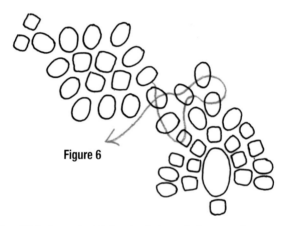

Figure 6

Step 15: String 1 size 8°. Pass back through the second strung size 8° of Step 14. Pass through the top position size 8° of the neck strap. Weave the thread back through the connection beads and into the pendant to secure. Trim close to work.

Step 16: Weave the other thread back through the connection beads that were just added and back through the pendant to secure. Cut the thread. Repeat for the other side.

ATTACHING LINKING SECTION

Step 17: Position the neck strap section with the attached pendant to the left, the linking section, with the 5 x 7 bead edge facing up, to the right.

Step 18: Using the thread from the linking section, string 1 size 8°. Pass through the size 11° of the pendant (as indicated on Figure 6). String 1 size 8°, pass through the top size 8 of the pendant.

Step 19: Pass back through the size 8° that is directly above the top bead of the pendant. String 2 size 8's and pass through the size 8° of the linking section. Repeat for the other side.

ATTACHING CENTER PENDANT

Step 20: Position the left linking section so that the 5 x 7 edge is up. String 2 size 8's and pass through the top size 8° of the remaining pendant. String 2 size 8's and pass through the top size 8° of the right linking section. String 3 size 8's and pass through the top size 8° of the left linking section. Weave through the piece to secure, then trim close to the piece (Figure 7). Repeat the thread motion, reversing the path, for the right linking section.

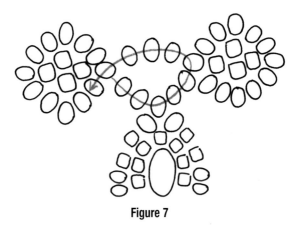

Figure 7

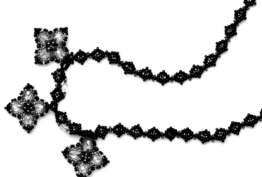

S. Raven Willey has hosted several bead retreats and workshops in southwestern Pennsylvania and has plans for more in the future. You can contact Raven through her website www.howlingrabbit.com.

Spiral Sync

Dustin Wedekind
Furnaceworked bead by Connie Haute

Materials
Size 8° seed beads
Size 15° seed beads (A)
Size 11° seed beads (B)
3mm pearls, stones, or crystals (C)
Focal bead
Large accent beads
Soft Flex .019" beading wire
Clasp
Crimp beads
Beading thread

Notions
Size 12 sharps beading needle
Crimping pliers
Scissors

This spiral variation is worked on a prestrung necklace. By using Soft Flex wire, you can string larger heavier beads that have small holes without the fear of breaking the thread.

Step 1: String a crimp bead and one side of the clasp on the end of the wire. Pass back through the crimp bead. Squeeze the bead with a pliers leaving a 1" tail. String approximately 2" of 8° seed beads, 1 accent bead, another 2" of seed beads, another accent bead, etc. for the length of your necklace. You can vary the number of seed beads in each section, but mirror them for the second half of the necklace after stringing the accent bead. Attach the other half of the clasp. Thread the 1" tail into the beads.

Step 2: Using 1 yard of thread, begin spiral stitch next to your focal bead. Pass through the first 8° bead and string 4 A. Slide the beads down to the necklace and tie a square knot, leaving a 3" tail. Pass through the 8° bead again and string 4 A. Pass through the same 8° and the next one on the wire (Figure 1). Flip the loops to the left.

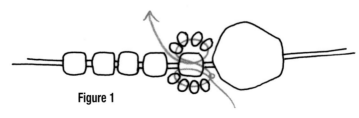

Figure 1

Step 3: String 2 A, 2 B, and 2 A and pass through the two base beads again. Repeat, passing through the two base beads plus one more. Flip the loops to the left.

Step 4: String 2 A, 4 B, and 2 A and pass through the three base beads. Repeat, passing through the three base beads plus one more. Flip the loops to the left.

Step 5: String 2 A, 2 B, 1 C, 2 B, and 2 A and pass through the four base beads. Repeat, stringing a size 8° bead in place of the C bead and passing through the four base beads plus one more. Flip the loops to the left.

Step 6: Repeat Step 5, working two loops over four base beads and then shifting up one bead to work another two loops over four base beads (Figure 2).

Step 7: When you reach the last four beads of a section, work Steps 4–2 backward. After the last A beads are stitched, pass the thread through one of the longer loops exiting the last bead, tie a knot between beads, then pass through the base beads and repeat. Trim the thread at the base of the spiral. Repeat for the beginning tail.

Figure 2

Step 8: Repeat Steps 2–7 for each section of the necklace. Don't cheat by passing through an accent bead to start the next section—the friction of the heavy bead rubbing against the wire will break the thread. At the end sections, pass a loop of seed beads through the clasp to camouflage the crimp and wire.

Note: If your base beads become crowded, you can carefully break one or two of them off the wire.

Dustin Wedekind is the managing editor of Beadwork® magazine.

Pearl Net Choker

Linda Richmond

Materials

Six 16" strands of 3.5–4mm small button or
　　round pearls
Delicas in color to complement pearls
Size 15° seed beads in color to complement pearls
Two 8–12mm bead caps
Hook and eye clasp
Size 0 Nymo beading thread in color to
　　complement beads

Notions

Size 15 beading needles
Scissors
Glue or nail polish
Needle-nose pliers or needle gripper
Beeswax

This choker uses variations of horizontal netting. By changing
the number and size of the pearls, seed beads, and stitches,
many variations are possible using the same basic technique.

PEARL NETTING

Round 1: Using 1 yard of doubled waxed thread and leaving a
6" tail, *string 1 pearl, 1 Delica, 1 size 15°, and 1 Delica. Repeat
from * eleven times. Use a square knot to tie the thread into a
circle. Pass through the next Delica, size 15°, Delica, and pearl
to position your needle for the next round. Note: Size 15 beading needles are very fragile, so always hold your thread to pull
it through beads; don't use your needle to pull your thread.

Round 2: String 1 Delica, 1 size 15°, 1 Delica, 1 pearl, 1 Delica, 1 size 15°, and 1 Delica. Pass through the second pearl of
the first round (Figure 1). Repeat this pattern for the rest of
this round, passing through every other pearl. After passing
through the last pearl of the first round, pass through the
Delica, size 15°, Delica, and pearl of this round to make a
"step up."

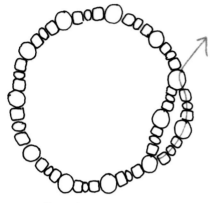

Round 3: String 1 Delica, 1 size 15°, 1 Delica, 1 pearl, 1 Delica, 1 size 15°, and 1 Delica. Pass through the next pearl (you no longer skip a pearl). Continue until you finish this round and complete the step up.

Repeat Round 3 until you run out of pearls.

Figure 1

SEED BEAD NETTING

Step 1: Measure the length you'd like your choker to be and subtract the length of the pearl netting portion you just completed. Following the instructions below will give you 1⅝" of netting for each side, plus another 1" for the caps and hook and eye. By adjusting your numbers a bit you can decide whether you should do the number of rounds given in each step below or do more or fewer rounds in each step to achieve your desired length.

Step 2: Round 1: String 3 Delicas, 1 size 15°, and 3 Delicas. Pass through the next pearl. Continue this step until you finish the round. Complete the round with a step up by passing through 3 Delicas and a size 15°.

Round 2: String 3 Delicas, 1 size 15°, and 3 Delicas. Pass through the next size 15°. Continue until you finish this round and step up to the next.

Round 3: Repeat Round 2.

Rounds 4–12: String 2 Delicas, 1 size 15°, and 2 Delicas. Step up to prepare for the next round each time.

Rounds 13–18: String 1 Delica, 1 size 15°, and 1 Delica. Step up to prepare for the next round each time. Your thread should be exiting a size 15° bead after completing Round 18 (Figure 2).

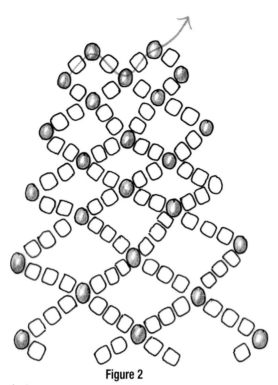

Figure 2

BEAD CAP AND CLASP

Step 1: Pass through the bead cap, through the hook, and back through the bead cap. Ease the cap down over the bead-work, and pull the thread fairly tight over the hook.

Pass through another size 15° and up through the cap, through the hook, and back through the cap. Keep the cap even over the beadwork, snugging the thread evenly and tight over the hook. Continue passing through the size 15°s, up through the cap, through the hook, and back through the cap until you have passed through all the 15° beads. Weave in all working and tail threads. Tie knots to secure, seal with glue or nail polish, and trim close to work.

Step 2: Repeat Step 1 for the other side with the other cap and the eye portion of your hook and eye closure.

Linda Richmond of Santa Fe, New Mexico, has been captivated by beads for most of her life, and she launched a full-time beading career in 1995. She sells her kits, along with beads, tools, books, and supplies, through her website at www.lindarichmond.com.

Knotty Necklace

Diane Fitzgerald

Materials

Forty-five to fifty 6–10mm beads (crystals,
   pressed glass, lampworked, etc.)
100 size 11° seed beads in color to complement
   the larger beads
3 yards of size FF, FFF, #18 cord or one card of 72"
   beadcord with needle (check to be sure the cord
   will pass once through your seed bead and three
   strands through your large bead)
Size B or finer Nymo beading thread

Notions

Scissors
T-pin
Size 12 beading needle
Watch crystal cement (G-S Hypo Cement)
Nail polish

This simple necklace
can be worn in a
number of ways:
looped twice or three
times around your
neck; folded in half
twice, twisted, and
secured with a ring
closure; folded in
half three times and
worn as a bracelet
with a ring closure;
or just as is, long
and loose.

Step 1: Coat one end of the cord with clear nail polish and let dry to stiffen. Make an overhand knot 6" from the end of the cord. String 1 seed bead, 1 larger bead, and 1 seed bead. Snug the beads close to the knot and tie another knot close to the last seed bead strung. Insert a t-pin in the loop of the knot and, while holding the cord, push the t-pin toward the bead to tighten.

Step 2: Make another knot 1" to 1½" away from the last knot and string the same sequence of seed bead, larger bead, and seed bead. Snug with a knot. Tie another knot 1" to 1½" away from the last knot. Repeat until the necklace measures 72" to 84".

Step 3: Knot the ends together with a square knot between a seed bead and a large bead. Set aside.

BURYING THE CORD ENDS

Step 4: Cut a 10" length of Nymo. Thread it through the needle and tie the ends with a square knot. Dab the knot with nail polish so it doesn't come undone. Allow to dry. Pass the needle and most of the thread through the bead so only a loop of thread is still extending. Place one of the cord ends through the loop then pull the loop through the bead (Figure 1). Do the same with the remaining cord end.

Figure 1

Make the final knot by doing the first half of a square knot, then passing the ends around the cord, and doing a complete square knot. Saturate the knot with glue. Clip the ends near the knot.

Diane Fitzgerald is a bead artist, writer, and teacher who lives in Minneapolis, Minnesota. She can be reached at dmfbeads@bitstream.net.

Green Temple

Judi Mullins

Materials

Focal bead
Assortment of pressed glass, crystal, metal, and
    semi-precious beads
Size 6°, 8°, 11°, and 15° seed beads
Size D Nymo or Silamide beading thread
20-gauge wire
12" of ⅜"–¼" chain
2 crimp beads
Soft Flex .019" beading wire

Notions

Wire cutter
Size 12 beading needle
Glue
Scissors
Round-nose pliers
Needle-nose pliers
Crimping pliers

This twisting, curving snake-like necklace is certain to snag
attention.

Step 1: Cut a length of chain that is slightly longer than you
want the choker section of your necklace to be. You will leave
at least a few links of chain at each end open.

Step 2: Tie a piece of thread three links in from one end of
the chain. Glue this knot for extra strength. Weave in and
out of the links adding size 6° or 8° seed beads in each link
(Figure 1). Continue until you reach three links from the
other end and tie another knot to anchor the thread. This is
your base row of beads.

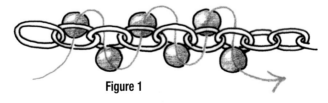

Figure 1

Step 3: Work back toward the beginning, again adding beads
in each link. Do not add the beads in exactly the same place as

the first row. Pass back and forth adding beads a few times until you have a nice base row to work from.

Step 4: Add larger beads. Spread them along the necklace and add smaller beads in between. Work in three dimensions and keep the diameter of the rope the same all along its width.

Step 5: Begin to use other beads for your anchors rather than always using your base row. Look for open spaces where the chain shows through and cover these spaces with beads. Use smaller and smaller size beads as you create more layers. Continue adding beads until you have a nice lush rope with no open holes or gaps.

Step 6: String a piece of 20-gauge wire through the focal bead. Make a hangman's-noose loop at the top and bottom of the bead. Sew the desired type of fringe through the bottom loop. Attach a piece of thread to the center of the necklace where you want your focal bead to be. Pass through the wrapped loop at the top of the focal bead and attach it securely to the necklace by sewing into the rope and through the wrapped loop several times.

Step 7: Cut the chain so that you have only a single link protruding from the bead rope on each end.

Step 8: Cut a length of Soft Flex. String 1 crimp bead and pass the wire through the last remaining link on the rope. Pass back through the crimp bead and squeeze it with a crimping pliers, leaving a 1" tail. String a bead with a large enough hole to fit over the crimp bead snugly up against the end of the beaded rope. String more beads until you have enough to reach the point where you want to put the clasp. String a second crimp bead and one side of the clasp. Pass back through the crimp beads and as many rope beads as possible. Pull tight and squeeze the second crimp bead. Cut the wire close to the beads.

Repeat Step 8 for the other side of necklace.

Judi Mullins has been doing beadwork off and on for most of her adult life. She has been published in several magazines and has taught around the Northwest area. She is now teaching classes and doing beadwork designs out of her home in Tigard, Oregon. You can contact her at bead.garden@verizon.net.

Turned Wire

Deb Dzuris

Materials

35 round 6mm olivine Japanese glass pearls
26-gauge gold wire
7 round 4mm olivine Japanese glass pearls
One 2mm gold bead
1 small gold disk
Two 6 to 8mm gold bead caps
8" of tiny gold chain
5 heavy-gauge 6mm gold jump rings
2 oval gold jump rings
One 10mm gold lobster clasp

Notions

Wire cutter
Round-nose pliers
Needle-nose pliers

This is a great project for beginning wire turners. The rough, imperfect nature of the loops complements the old-style look of the necklace.

Step 1: Using a 6mm bead and the 26-gauge wire, make a hangman's noose loop. Make a hangman's noose loop on the other side of the bead.

Step 2: Use the 26-gauge wire to make a hangman's noose loop, but this time incorporate one of the loops created in the previous step (Figure 1). String a 6mm bead and finish the other side of the bead with a hangman's noose loop.

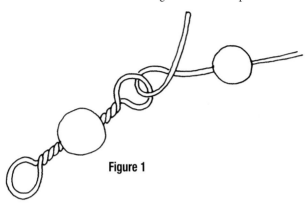

Figure 1

Step 3: Repeat Step 2 until you have a chain seventeen beads long.

Step 4: Repeat Steps 1–3.

Step 5: Cut seven lengths of chain in varying lengths from ½" to 1½".

Step 6: *Make a hangman's noose loop incorporating one end of one of the pieces of chain cut in Step 5. String a 4mm bead. Snug the bead to the loop and cut about ½" away from the bead. Bend the wire to the bead. Repeat from * six times.

Step 7: Make a hangman's noose loop using the 26-gauge wire and incorporate the other end of each piece of chain cut in Step 5. String a bead cap, a 6mm, a bead cap, a small gold disk, and the 2mm gold bead. Finish the other side of the bead with a hangman's noose loop.

Step 8: Open a 6mm jump ring and string on the pendant created in Steps 5–7 and each neck strap created in Steps 1–4. Close the jump ring.

Step 9: Open a 6mm jump ring and string on one end of one neck strap and another 6mm jump ring. Close the jump ring. Repeat for the other strap.

Step 10: Open an oval jump ring and string it through the last 6mm jump ring strung and one side of the clasp. Close the jump ring. Repeat for the other strap.

Deb Dzuris is the proprietor of 4th Street Bead, 118 East 4th Street, Loveland, CO 80537.

Topaz Beauty

Pat Mayer

Sparkly Wheel designed by Nikia Angel

Materials
27 bicone 4mm Austrian crystals
17 AB round 6mm or 8mm Austrian crystals
Thirty-two 5mm or 6mm rondelles with coordinating
or matching crystals
1 round 4mm Austrian crystal
1 large faceted vertical-hole drop crystal
Size 11° Japanese seed beads or Delicas
Size B Nymo beading thread
32" of size .019" Soft Flex wire or 20# Power Pro
Clasp
2 crimp beads

Notions
Size 11 or 12 needle
Beeswax or thread conditioner
Crimping pliers
Wire cutter
Scissors

Combine simple peyote tubes, crystal beads, and a swirling crystal wheel to make this stunning topaz necklace.

Note: Instructions are for a 16" necklace. For each extra inch of necklace length, add one additional crystal, one peyote tube, and two rondelles.

SPARKLY WHEEL

Step 1: Using 2½' of doubled waxed thread, string a tension bead. String 9 sets of one 4mm crystal and 3 size 11°. Remove the tension bead. Tie into a circle with a square knot, leaving an 8" tail.

Step 2: Working from right to left, pass through the center bead of the three 11°. *String 5 size 11° and pass through the center bead of the next set of size 11° (Figure 1). Repeat from * around the circle, keeping the work tight. Weave to the center bead of the first set of size 11° you added in this step.

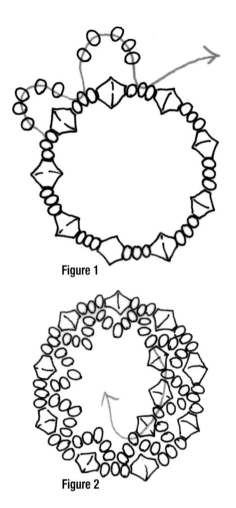

Figure 1

Figure 2

Step 3: *String one 4mm crystal and pass through the center bead of the next set of 5 size 11° (Figure 2).

Repeat from * around the circle to add a total of 9 crystals, gently pushing this circle toward the inside of the circle created in Step 2. Weave back up to the center bead of the size 11° added in the first step.

Step 4: Repeat Step 2. Weave to the center bead of the first set of 5 added in this step.

Step 5: Repeat Step 3. Pull everything tight and secure with an overhand knot. Do not cut the thread.

Step 6: String 1 size 11°, one 4mm crystal, 1 rondelle, one 6mm or 8mm crystal, 1 rondelle, the drop crystal, and either 1 or 3 size 11°. Skipping the last size 11°, pass through all again, except the first size 11°. String another size 11° and weave the thread through the wheel to secure; tie off and cut all threads.

Peyote Tubes

Make 14.

Using 20" of doubled, waxed thread, string a tension bead. String 8 size 11° and work even count peyote for 8 rows. Tail and working threads must be exiting from opposite corners. Roll into a small tight tube and sew up the edges. Weave in the working and tail threads, tie a knot, weave into a few more beads to hide the knot, and trim close to work.

Assembly

Step 1: Use the beading wire or Power Pro to string one crimp bead and half the clasp. Pass back through the crimp bead and snug the bead up to the clasp. Crimp the bead with a pliers.

Step 2: String one 6mm or 8mm crystal, 1 rondelle, 1 peyote tube, 1 rondelle, one 6mm or 8mm crystal, 1 rondelle, etc., until you've reached half your desired length. String the Sparkly Wheel by passing the wire through the three-bead set (size 11°, crystal, size 11°) on the outside of the wheel, just opposite the drop. Continue beading the other half of the necklace to mirror the first side. Add a crimp bead and other side of the clasp as you did in Step 1.

Pat Mayer divides her time between Florida and traveling with her husband in a motor home. Among the many joys that have come to her through beading are the love of the creative process, the beauty of the beads, the fun of the hunt, and the wonderful friendships made with kindred spirits she has met along the beading path.

Victorian Necklace

Lisa Norris

Materials

Size 11° gold Delicas
Size 11° bronze Delicas
10–20mm topaz crystal and brass ornament
12 bicone 5mm AB topaz Swarovski crystals
Size B Nymo beading thread
French bullion or gimp
Clasp

Notions

Size 12 beading or sharps needle
Scissors

Create this elegant necklace by adding a swirl of picots and loops to peyote-stitched strips.

Step 1: Using 2 yards of thread and leaving an 8" tail, string a tension bead. Make a peyote strip two beads wide by first stringing 2 beads. Let the beads slide down to the tension bead. Pass back through the tension bead. Adjust the beads just strung so that the third bead sits on top of the second bead. String 1 bead. Pass through the second bead just strung (Figure 1). Continue adding one bead and passing back through the last bead strung until the strip is the desired length of your necklace (15"–16").

Step 2: String ⅓" of the French bullion and one side of the clasp. Pass through the last bead added so that the wire makes a loop. Repeat on the other end with the tail.

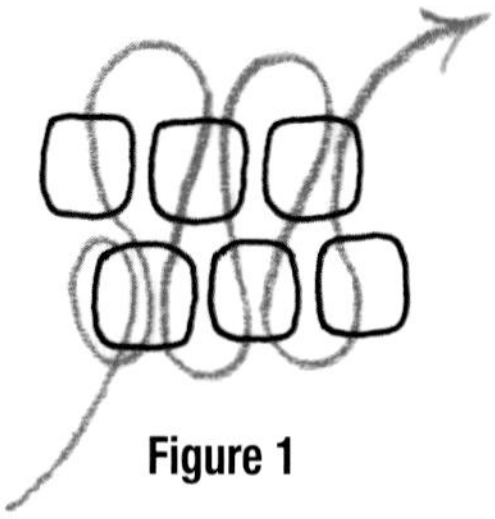

Figure 1

Step 3: Repeat Step 1 to make an 8"–9" peyote strip two beads wide. Finish each end of the strip by adding 5–6 beads with ladder stitch. Each end should have its ladder-stitched portion on the same side (top).

Step 4: Lay the first strip in a circle. Place the center of the shorter strip 1" below the center of the longer one. Curve the shorter strip up to meet the longer one. Sew the last 3 beads of the ladders to the longer strip.

Step 5: Work a series of bronze picots and loops from the point of attachment back to the clasp (Figure 2). Make a picot by stringing 4 beads, passing back through the first bead, and then passing through the bead on the peyote strip next to the bead you exited to start the picot. Pass through the bead that sits below/between the two top beads so your needle travels in a triangle shape—two beads up and one down.

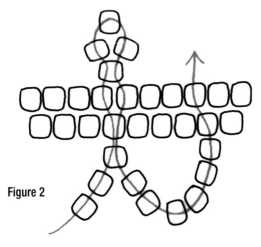

Figure 2

Make a loop by stringing 8 beads, skipping three beads on the peyote strip, and passing through the fourth bead. When you pass up through the peyote, make sure your needle is angled so that when the next picot is made, the bottom bead of the picot will be directly above the top bead of the loop.

Repeat for the other side of the necklace.

Step 6: Begin a new thread and exit 3 peyote-strip beads down from the first picot made in Step 5. Start a series of picots and loops, but gradually increase the distance between loops. Use 6 bronze for loops 1–4, and skip 3 beads on the peyote strip between each loop. Use 4 bronze, 1 crystal, and 4 bronze for loops 5–7 and skip 4 beads on the peyote strip. Use 5 bronze, 1 crystal, and 5 bronze for loops 8 and 9 and skip 5 beads on the peyote strip. For the tenth loop, use 16 bronze and skip 6 beads on the peyote strip.

Work in reverse order to the other side of the necklace.

Step 7: Work your thread to the lower peyote strip, three beads away from the ladder-stitched portion. Make a picot and pass through the peyote strip into the center of the necklace.

String 1 bronze and pass through the center two beads of the opposing loop. String 2 bronze. Skipping 3 beads, pass through the lower peyote strip and make a picot on the opposite side. String 2 bronze and pass through the center two beads of the opposing loops. String 2 bronze, skip 3 beads, and pass through the lower strip and make a picot.

Use 3 bronze for Loop 3, passing through the center two beads of the opposing loop and skipping 4 beads on the peyote strip. Use 3 bronze for Loop 4, passing through the crystal of the opposing loop and skipping 4 beads on the peyote strip. Use 4 beads for Loop 5, passing through the crystal and skipping 5 beads on the peyote strip. Use 5 beads for Loop 6, passing through the crystal and skipping 5 beads. Use 6 beads for Loop 7, skipping 5 beads on the peyote strip. Use 7 beads for Loop 8, skipping 6 beads. Use 8 beads for Loop 9, skipping 6 beads. For Loop 10, string 7 beads and pass through the middle two beads of the opposing loop. String 7 and skip 7 beads on the peyote strip.

Work the loops in reverse order.

Step 8: Sew the crystal ornament to the center loop. Weave in all working and tail threads and trim close to the work.

Lisa Norris is a self-taught beadworker with a degree in chemical engineering, which she hasn't used since her kids were born. She teaches beading in northern Virginia and sells her work in shops in Virginia and Arizona.

Growing Vine

Doris Coghill

Materials

Assortment of flower and leaf beads
Assortment of size 6° seed beads, 7mm glass beads,
    and various accent beads or crystals
5 yards of 26-gauge wire
4 crimp tubes
10–16" of Soft Flex .014" beading wire
Clasp
2 split rings

Notions

Wire cutter
Needle-nose pliers
Crimping pliers

Make this easy necklace much as you would a wreath for your door. Except you get to show off this wreath wherever you go.

Step 1: Choose a large leaf bead for the center front of the necklace. String this bead and slide it to the center of one 3-yard length of 26-gauge wire. Twist the wire for ⅛–¼", down close to the bead. Make the twist by holding the two pieces of wire with one hand and the leaf bead with the wire through it in the other hand. Continue adding beads, or multiple bead clusters, to each end of the wire. Add the beads close together and twist after adding each one (Figure 1).

After every two or three beads or clusters, twist the individual twists together to give the piece body and get the twists close together. After completing 1"–2" of twists, decide which side of the group of twists will be the front of your necklace and arrange the twists so the beads are all facing up. You have now completed the focal section of the necklace.

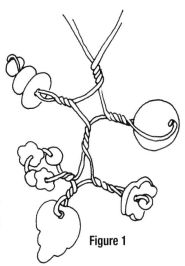

Figure 1

Step 2: Add the second piece (2 yards) of wire by twisting the middle of it around the wire directly above the focal section of the necklace. Split the four pieces of wire so that two will go up each side of the necklace (Figure 2).

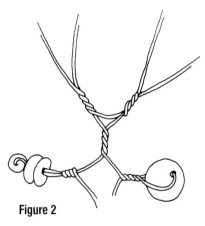

Figure 2

Continue adding beads or bead clusters, twisting after each one, until the necklace is the desired length. Consider spacing the twisted beads in the strap section farther apart than the ones in the center focal section.

Note: If you have trouble twisting, try a needle-nose pliers. Hold it gently because twisting the wire too tightly will break the wire. If your wire does break, wrap the broken end around the adjacent wrapped bead stem. Lay the remaining piece of wire back about ¾" from the wrap and twist it securely around the stem of several wrapped beads, then continue as before.

Step 3: Switch from the wire twisting to the strung part of the necklace by making a cluster of twists and then finishing it with a small loop behind the cluster as close to the base as possible. Wrap the wire back around itself to secure and cut off the excess, making sure the ends of the wire are buried within the work. Cut a piece of Soft Flex the desired length to finish the necklace plus 2". String a crimp tube and pass through the loop you just created under the last cluster. Pass back through the crimp tube leaving a ½" tail. Use the crimping pliers to flatten the crimp tube. Arrange the twisted clusters so they cover the crimp tube. String beads to the desired length, being sure to cover the tail wire at the beginning of the strand. Attach a clasp the same way you attached the Soft Flex to the loop below the cluster being sure to put the split ring onto the Soft Flex loop before you fasten the crimp. Attach your clasp to the split ring. Repeat for the other side.

Doris Coghill has been working with seed beads for about nine years, but has been involved with some type of crafts all her life. She is currently busy with designing and teaching beadwork and working with her business, Dee's Place. She can be reached at www.beadsbydee.com.

Pearl Sautoir

Arlene Baker

Materials

Two 60" strands of round 2mm plastic pearls
One 60" strand of 78 round 3.5mm plastic pearls
40 round 7mm plastic pearls
39 rice-shaped 8mm x 4mm plastic pearls
Liquid Rit dye in scarlet, dark brown, and yellow
Size B Nymo beading thread in color to match pearls
        after they are dyed

Notions

Plastic or glass bowl
#10 twisted-steel wire beading needles
Scissors
Tape measure
Beeswax

This pearl necklace or sautoir is similar to a design from the 1920s. In Virginia Snow's *Authority on Bead Bags, Necklaces, etc. Book No. 29*, 1926, it was described as a novelty pearl chain.

Step 1: Dye the pearls for a cultured-pearl look. Mix 1 tablespoon of yellow, ⅛ teaspoon of scarlet, and 1 drop of dark brown. Add 2 quarts of hot water. The color of the dye bath should be rusty orange. Keep the water hot by reheating in a microwave if necessary. Dye all the pearls at the same time in the same bath so the dye lot stays the same. Be sure to submerge each strand completely. Keep the pearls in the dye bath until the color is pleasing to you. When you're finished, rinse the pearls in cool water and hang to dry. Note: Because the pearls are different sizes, the color may not look exact, but when the necklace is made they will match perfectly.

Step 2: Measure 100" of conditioned thread and string the needle, pulling it to the center of the thread. Use one end of the thread to string one 7mm and make a tension bead. Do the same on the other end of the thread.

Step 3: *String one 7mm, one 3.5mm, 1 rice, and one 3.5. Repeat from * 18 times. String one 3.5mm, 1 rice, one 3.5mm, one 3.5mm, 1 rice, one 3.5mm. *String one 7mm, one 3.5mm, 1 rice, and one 3.5. Repeat from * 18 times. String one 3.5mm, 1 rice, and one 3.5mm. Leave at least a 5" tail on each end so the pearls can slide easily. Tie a knot close to the ends to form a circle with an 8" gap between the pearls. Trim the thread above the knot and remove the needle and the two 7mms.

Step 4: Tie a wire needle to the end of a 50" length of conditioned thread. Tape one end of the thread to the knotted end of the beads strung in Step 3. Put another piece of tape over the knot and new thread and temporarily anchor all to the work surface.

Step 5: Pass through the 7mm, the 3.5mm, and the rice pearl first strung in Step 3. *String five 2mm. Pass back through the rice pearl and pull your thread tight (Figure 1). Repeat from * 5 times. Pass through the next 3.5mm. After you've completed a few rice pearls feel free to remove the taped piece from your work station.

Step 6: Repeat Step 5 eighteen times until you reach the middle of the necklace.

Step 7: String two 7mm and fifty-six 2mm. *Pass back through the 7mm and pull the thread tight. Pass your thread over the thread between the two 3.5mm. Repeat from * twice.

Step 8: Pass through the next 3.5mm on the necklace and repeat Step 5 nineteen times until you reach the top of the necklace.

Figure 1

Step 9: Tie any working and tail threads and secure the knots with glue. Hide any thread ends by rethreading them through the pearls and trim close to work.

Arlene Baker is a frequent contributor to Beadwork®. *She is the author of* Beads in Bloom*, published by Interweave Press, and she's a popular teacher nationwide. Arlene can be reached at (562) 928-3583.*

Silver Twister

Suzanne Helwig

Materials

1½ oz. of 21-gauge sterling-silver square soft wire
Large silver accent beads
Blue recycled faceted glass beads
Size 6° clear seed beads
2 silver crimp beads
2 heavy gauge silver jump rings
32" of Soft Flex .024" clear beading wire
Silver clasp

Notions

Wire cutter
Twist 'n' Curl with small round dowel
Crimping pliers

This necklace is a true head turner. The components are fairly simple to make, and assembly is a breeze.

Step 1: Use the square wire to make six simple 1½" Twist 'n' Curl twisted beads following the manufacturer's directions. Bend beads into a curved shape as shown.

Step 2: Use the Soft Flex to string one crimp bead. Pass through one of the jump rings and back through the crimp bead leaving a 2" tail. Snug the crimp bead up to the jump ring and squeeze tight.

Step 3: String 2 size 6°, 1 recycled, 2 size 6°, 1 recycled, 2 size 6°, *1 recycled, 1 silver, 1 recycled, 1 twisted. Repeat from * five times. String 1 recycled, 1 silver, 1 recycled, 2 size 6°, 1 recycled, 2 size 6°, 1 recycled, 2 size 6°, and 1 crimp bead. Pass through the other jump ring, back through the crimp bead, and through as many of the beads just strung as possible. Snug the wire to take out any slack and squeeze the crimp bead.

Step 4: Attach the clasp to the jump rings.

Suzanne Helwig is a jewelry designer for WigJig, the inventors of the original transparent wire jigs. Reach her at www.wigjig.com.

Split River

Jean Campbell

Materials
Size 1 blue irid bugles
Thirteen 6mm Montana blue bicone Swarovski crystals
Twenty-one 3mm lavender round Swarovski crystals
Silver 3-hole clasp

Notions
Size 12 beading or sharps needle
Scissors
Ruler

This elegant necklace gently glides along your body line and ends in a splash of crystals.

Step 1: Using a yard of thread and leaving a 6" tail, make an 8½" length of peyote stitch 4 bugle beads wide. When you reach 8½", start beading 2-beads wide (Figure 1) on the right side for 3". Create the strip so that the "up" bead is on the right as you look at the thin strip pointing up. Exit from the second-to-last bead added.

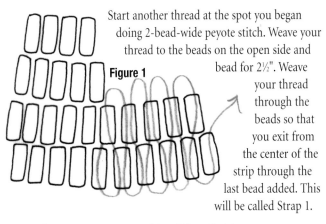

Start another thread at the spot you began doing 2-bead-wide peyote stitch. Weave your thread to the beads on the open side and bead for 2½". Weave your thread through the beads so that you exit from the center of the strip through the last bead added. This will be called Strap 1.

Figure 1

Step 2: Repeat Step 1. This will be called Strap 2.

Step 3: Make sure you have at least an 8" working thread on Strap 1. Use the thread of the longer 2-bead-wide length on Strap 1 to string one 3mm, one 6mm, one 3mm, one 6mm, one 3mm, one 6mm, one 3mm. Pass through the middle of the longer length on Strap 2 (Figure 2). Exit at the center of Strap 2.

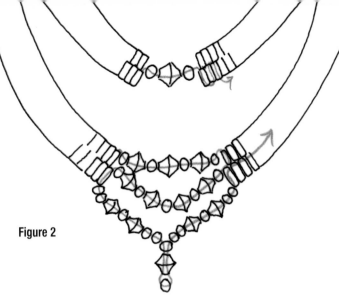

Figure 2

Step 4: String one 3mm, one 6mm, one 3mm, one 6mm, one 3mm, one 6mm, one 3mm, one 6mm, and one 3mm. Pass through the middle of Strap 1 (Figure 2).

Step 5: String two 3mm, one 6mm, one 3mm, one 6mm, three 3mm, one 6mm, and one 3mm. Pass back through the last 6mm strung. String two 3mm, one 6mm, one 3mm, one 6mm, and two 3mm. Pass through the outside bead of Strap 2 (Figure 2). Weave your thread up through Strap 2 to secure and trim close to work.

Use the working tail of Strap 2 to weave through all the crystals and Strap 1 to secure and trim close to work.

Step 6: Use the working tail of the short 2-bead peyote length on Strap 1 to string one 3mm, one 6mm, and one 3mm. Pass through the middle of the short length on Strap 2 (Figure 2). Weave up through Strap 2 to secure and trim close to work.

Use the working tail of Strap 2 to weave through the crystals and Strap 1 to secure and trim close to work.

Leaf Fringe Conversation

Linda Gettings

Materials

85–100 cube beads or 200 bugle beads
Seventy 10mm tube beads
60 faceted 5 or 6mm fire-polished beads
180 faceted 3 or 4mm fire-polished beads
Assortment of size 6°, 8°, and 11° seed beads to
    complement other beads
Assortment of lampworked beads
Size D beading thread

Notions

Size 12 beading needles
Scissors

If you're a fringe lover like Linda, get ready to bead up a storm to make this substantial necklace. The collar portion can be made with either cubes or bugles, and the fringe is largely up to you.

Step 1: Using a yard of thread with a needle at each end, string 3 seed beads, one side of the clasp, 3 seed beads, and 1 cube with one needle. Slide to the middle of the thread and pass through all again to make a circle and tie a knot.

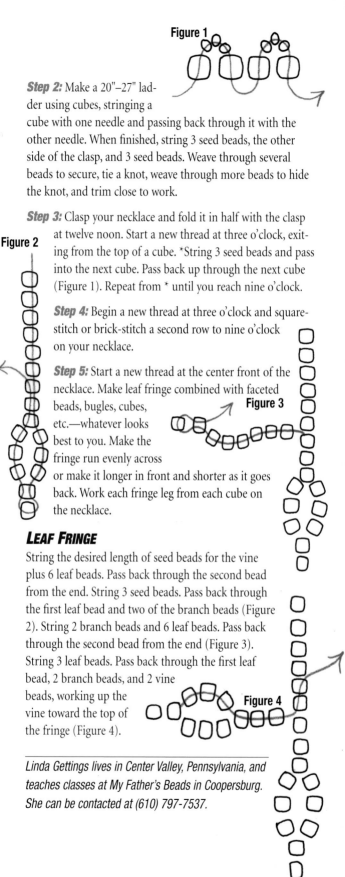

Figure 1

Step 2: Make a 20"–27" ladder using cubes, stringing a cube with one needle and passing back through it with the other needle. When finished, string 3 seed beads, the other side of the clasp, and 3 seed beads. Weave through several beads to secure, tie a knot, weave through more beads to hide the knot, and trim close to work.

Step 3: Clasp your necklace and fold it in half with the clasp at twelve noon. Start a new thread at three o'clock, exiting from the top of a cube. *String 3 seed beads and pass into the next cube. Pass back up through the next cube (Figure 1). Repeat from * until you reach nine o'clock.

Figure 2

Step 4: Begin a new thread at three o'clock and square-stitch or brick-stitch a second row to nine o'clock on your necklace.

Step 5: Start a new thread at the center front of the necklace. Make leaf fringe combined with faceted beads, bugles, cubes, etc.—whatever looks best to you. Make the fringe run evenly across or make it longer in front and shorter as it goes back. Work each fringe leg from each cube on the necklace.

Figure 3

LEAF FRINGE

String the desired length of seed beads for the vine plus 6 leaf beads. Pass back through the second bead from the end. String 3 seed beads. Pass back through the first leaf bead and two of the branch beads (Figure 2). String 2 branch beads and 6 leaf beads. Pass back through the second bead from the end (Figure 3). String 3 leaf beads. Pass back through the first leaf bead, 2 branch beads, and 2 vine beads, working up the vine toward the top of the fringe (Figure 4).

Figure 4

Linda Gettings lives in Center Valley, Pennsylvania, and teaches classes at My Father's Beads in Coopersburg. She can be contacted at (610) 797-7537.

One-To-Many Strand Necklace

Diane Fitzgerald

Materials

3 oz. multicolored size 9° to 11° seed beads
200–300 small beads, stone chips, rondelles,
    or size 6° or 8° seed beads
Nymo D beading thread
1½ yards of size F or FF bead cord
Clasp
2 clamshell bead tips

Notions

Piece of multicolored clothing or a picture
Tape
2 size 12 beading needles
Small sharp scissors
Clear nail polish
Lighter
Pencil
Paper
Small box about 4" x 4" x 1" deep
12" x 18" piece of cardboard
Fresh beeswax or microcrystalline wax

Use a favorite piece of multicolored clothing or a picture as a guide in choosing the bead colors for this necklace. Color mixing with seed beads, a process similar to mixing paint, is an important part of creating this piece.

Step 1: Use the piece of clothing or the picture's colors to guide you in assembling small quantities of seed beads in related colors. Mix ¼ to ½ cup of these beads together in a small dish by adding about a half-teaspoon at a time and watching how the color mixture shifts. Only add small amounts each time. Next, assemble approximately 200 small beads—rondelles, E beads, or stone chips in related colors in a separate dish.

Step 2: Cut two 24" pieces of size F bead cord and fold in half. Place them on a table so the folded ends are 13½" apart and tape them securely to the table. Point the loops toward each other.

Step 3: Thread a needle with 3 yards of thread. Bring ends together and knot with a double overhand knot. Clip the tails close to the knot and melt the knot slightly with a lighter. Wax the thread so that the two strands stick together.

Step 4: Attach the thread to the cord loop with a lark's head knot. Bring the knotted end of the thread near the cord loop. Separate the strands. Pass the needle between the two strands so that the knot is near the bead cord.

Figure 1

Step 5: Adding Seed Beads: String seed beads and after each needle-full, or about 1¼" of beads, add a small bead or stone chip. When the length of the strand is exactly long enough to reach the other loop, pass the needle through the loop and back through the last 2–3 beads just strung going in the opposite direction (Figure 1). Avoid adding a small bead near the bead cord loops because it will interfere with the way the strands hang.

Repeat Steps 3–5 until you have the desired number of strands for your necklace, usually twelve to twenty-four strands.

Step 6: After the desired number of strands are strung, remove the tape from the bead cord on one end and string 6½" of large, bold, solid color beads on the strands (both strands go through the large beads). Bring the two ends of the bead cord through a bead tip, tie with a square

ADDING NEW THREAD

Add a new thread in the middle of a strand rather than near the cord loops. Leave the old needle on the thread. Prepare a second needle and thread as you did the first. Pass the new needle through the last 4–6 beads just strung so that both needles are coming out of the same bead in the same direction. Tie the old and new threads together with a square knot. Apply clear nail polish to the knot. String more beads on the new thread. Later bring the old thread through several beads and clip the excess.

knot, and apply nail polish to the knot. Clip the excess cord and close the bead tip over the knot. Do the same with the cord on the other side. Attach one part of the clasp to each bead tip.

Diane Fitzgerald is a bead artist, writer, and teacher who lives in Minneapolis, Minnesota. She can be reached at dmfbeads@bitstream.net.

Ribbons

Chris Prussing

Materials

7 colors of pinch beads, 100 for each
    color (A, B, C, D, E, F, G)
4 strands of size 11˚ seed beads
10–12 yards of 10# test Power Pro

Notions

Hypo-tube cement
2 size 12 beading needles
Beading mat
Sharp scissors
Masking tape

The design possibilities of this simple technique are endless!
The basic necklace is a long ribbon of inch-wide beadwork
with the ends joined at a right angle.

Step 1: Using 5' of thread, string a needle on each end. For
the vertical pattern, string 1 B and let it fall to the center of the
thread. String a seed bead on each needle. On the right needle, string 1 C and a seed bead. On the left needle, string 1 A, a
seed bead, and 1 B. Cross the right needle through the B on
the left.

Figure 1

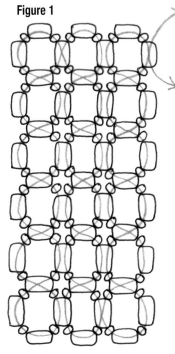

For the horizontal pattern,
string 1 A and let it fall to
the center of the thread. On
the right needle, string 1 A
and a seed bead. On the left
needle, string 1 A, 1 seed
bead, and 1 A. Cross the
right needle through the last
A on the left.

Step 2: Work three eighty-
unit-long rows of double-
needle right-angle weave
(Figure 1). Use a piece of
masking tape at the bottom
of the first row to keep the
beadwork in place on the
work surface.

The blocks of the horizontal pattern are worked as little U-shapes for the first half of the ribbon, then reversed for the second half. The sequence shown starts with 3 strips of each color, then 2 strips of each color, reversing to 2 strips of each color, then 3, and ending with 4 strips of G. G beads are also used to join the two ends.

Step 3: Once the ribbon is complete with the thread exiting from the side of the third row, bring the other end around (be careful not to twist it) and butt it up against the end of the third row. Use the threads from the end of the third row to add an additional row to connect the two ends (Figure 2). Then work into the body of the necklace, tie a knot, and pass through several beads and pull tight to hide the knot.

Figure 2

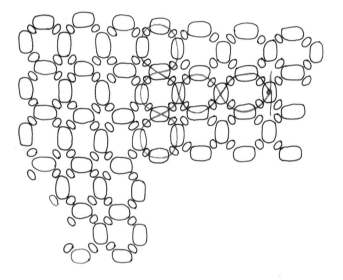

When you're joining the ends, select beads to maintain the color pattern or use different accent beads. The diagrams show the relationship between the center of the necklace and the joining beads.

Chris Prussing is a bead artist who can be contacted at www.rightangleweave.com.

Byzantine King

JoAnn Allard

Materials

Size 8° wheat Japanese seed beads
Size 8° topaz Japanese seed beads
Size 11° gold Japanese seed beads
49 topaz luster 6mm bell beads
49 topaz 6mm round beads
Fifteen 1½" brass head pins
6 topaz roses montees
Brass stamping
2 brass 6mm split rings
4 yards of #2 golden brown bead cord
Gold clasp

Notions

Quilt basting needle
Super Glue gel
Scissors
Round-nose pliers

A variation on the daisy chain, this necklace was inspired by jewelry designer Miriam Haskell, a lover of roses montees and dangles.

Step 1: Attach the two split rings to the top openings of the metal stamping. Glue the 6 roses montees to the center design.

Step 2: Using 2 yards of cord and leaving a 6" tail, string 3 topaz, one side of the clasp, and 3 topaz. Tie a knot to make a circle. Pass through all again and make a knot.

Step 3: String 1 wheat, 2 topaz, 2 wheat, 2 topaz, and 1wheat. Pass through all again and exit from the last wheat added. String 2 wheat and pass through the second wheat added in this step.

Step 4: String *2 topaz, 2 wheat, and 2 topaz. Pass through the bottom third wheat added in the last step. String 2 wheat. Pass through the second wheat added in this step. Repeat from * 28 times to make 8" (Figure 1). Don't cut the cord.

Figure 1

Step 5: Attach the chain to the stamping by passing through the split ring added to the stamping, the last daisy-chain section, the split ring again, and the 2 wheat farthest from the stamping.

Step 6: Pass back through the 2 wheat beads last strung and the second wheat added in the last chain. String 2 topaz, 1 bell, one 6mm, and 1 size 11° seed bead. Pass back through the 6mm, the bell, and the 2 topaz just strung. Pull up the slack. Pass through the wheat bead you last exited. *Pass through the middle wheat beads of the next daisy chain and the second bead added in that chain (Figure 2). String 2 topaz beads, 1 bell, one 6mm, and 1 size 11°. Pass back through the 6mm, bell, and 2 topaz beads. Pass through the wheat bead you last exited. Repeat from * 10 times.

Step 7: *Pass through the middle wheat beads of the next daisy chain and the second bead added in that chain (Figure 2). String 2 topaz beads, 1 bell, one 6mm, and 1 size 11°. Pass back through the 6mm, bell, and 2 topaz beads. Pass through the wheat bead you last exited. Repeat from * 6 times.

Figure 2

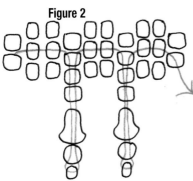

Step 8: Tie at least three knots between the beads. Pass through several beads to hide the knots and use glue to strengthen.

Step 9: Repeat Steps 2–8 for the other side of the necklace. Work in all tail and working threads and trim close to piece.

Step 10: Use the head pins to string one 6mm, 1 bell, and 1 topaz. Make a large loop on each one and fasten to the openings in the brass stamping.

JoAnn Allard is the founder of The Bead Tree in West Falmouth, Massachusetts. She is still beading and available by e-mail at beadtree@aol.com; www.thebeadtree.com.

Ruby Hitchhiker

Judi Wood

Materials
15–20 gr. size 11˚ metallic seed beads
5 gr. contrasting size 14˚ or 15˚ seed beads
48 Delicas in matching color to size 11˚s
8 faceted 3mm spacer rubies
Designer Findings' medium hollow tube
Silver safety clasp
2 silver 8mm jump rings
Size D Nymo beading thread or 10# Power Pro
3" of silver gimp

Notions
Size 12 beading needle
Sharp scissors or wire cutter (for Power Pro)

This uniquely stitched necklace harkens back to the Art Deco era. It is constructed in three sections—each strap is done with embellished brick and herringbone stitch, and a bead-covered hollow metal tube adorns the middle.

NECK STRAP
Step 1: Using a yard of thread and leaving an 8" tail, make an 8-Delica ladder. Connect the ends to make a ring. Work one round of brick stitch with Delicas. Work one round of herringbone stitch with Delicas (Figure 1). You will have four herringbone columns from the 8 Delica beads.

Figure 1

Step 2: Work one round of herringbone stitch with size 11˚s. After the first round, add a size 15˚ between each herringbone column (Figure 2). The hitchhiker is the size 15˚ bead in between each herringbone section. Work herringbone stitch, with the hitchhiker between each stitch, for eight rounds.

Figure 2

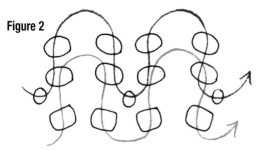

Step 3: After completing the eighth round, work the first column, then skip the second column and work the third, using a hitchhiker bead between the columns. After working the third column, skip to the first column. Work this middle section of two columns for three rows.

Step 4: Increase back to four rounds of herringbone by *stringing 1 hitchhiker, 2 size 11's, and 1 hitchhiker. Pass through the third column and work one stitch. Repeat from *, stitching into the first column. Work the second round using size 11's as the second and fourth columns. Work eight rounds.

Step 5: Repeat Steps 3 and 4 to complete 14 sections or 9".

Step 6: Use the tail thread to string ½" of gimp. Squeeze the first rounds together so that the bead you just exited is on the outside. Pass through the Delica directly opposite the bead you just exited. Pass up through the adjoining bead and string ½" of gimp. Pass through the Delica directly opposite. Pass through all again to secure. Tie a half hitch knot between beads, pass through a few more beads, and trim the tail close to the work. Attach a jump ring to all three lengths of gimp just added. Attach one side of the clasp to the jump ring.

Step 7: Repeat Steps 1–4 to create the other side of the strap.

FOCAL SECTION

Step 8: Create the final section by working a tube four columns wide in herringbone stitch off the end of your neck strap. Be sure to include the size 15° hitchhikers. Work the same amount for each strap so you will come up even when you insert the tube. Insert the tube in both ends and weave all four columns together around the tube. Sew two rubies in place where there is a space between the columns. Weave in the working threads, tie a half hitch knot between beads, pass through several more beads. Trim close to the work.

Award winning artist Judi Wood is a frequent contributor to Beadwork®. *Her work and show information can be seen at www.JudiWood.com.*

Va Va Voom

Jean Campbell

Materials

Two long tubes size 11° opaque black seed beads
Size 8° light blue irid seed beads
Size 2 silver-lined teal bugles
Size 1 opaque black bugles
Fifty 4mm teal Czech fire-polished faceted beads
7mm irid teal leaf beads with horizontal holes
Two spools size B or D black Nymo thread
Hefty clasp

Notions

Size 12 beading or sharps needle
Scissors
Measuring tape

Make this ruffly dangly jangly collar using netting, chain, and fringe techniques.

Step 1: Make a Victorian Chain. Begin by using a yard's length of thread and leaving a 10" tail with a tension bead attached. String 1 black, 1 blue, 1 black, 1 blue, and 3 black. Pass back through the second-to-last bead strung so that you form a pointed cap or picot on the string of beads (Figure 1).

Step 2: String 1 black, 1 blue, 1 black. Pass back through the first blue strung in Step 1.

Figure 1

Step 3: String 3 black. Pass back through the second-to-last bead strung to form a picot on the other side. String 1 black, 1 blue, 1 black. Pass back through the blue strung in the previous step.

Step 4: Rep Step 3 until you reach your neck measurement. When you attain the desired length, weave in the tail thread and working threads and trim close to the work.

Step 5: Start a new thread at the end of the Victorian Chain. Exit from the picot bead toward the length of the chain.

Step 6: String 2 black, 1 little bugle, 1 black, 1 little bugle, and 2 black. Pass through the next picot bead.

Step 7: Rep Step 6 for the length of the chain. When you've reached the end, weave your thread through the beads so you

exit from the black at the middle of the last net, ready to go in the opposite direction.

Step 8: String 1 blue, 1 large bugle, 1 black, 1 blue, 1 black, 1 large bugle, 1 blue. Pass through the black at the middle of the next net.

Step 9: Rep Step 8 for the length of the collar.

Step 10: After completing the last net, string 1 blue, 1 large bugle, 1 black, 1 blue, 1 black, 1 large bugle, 1 black, 1 blue, 1 black, 1 large bugle, and 1 black. Pass back through the blue at the middle of the last net created in this row.

Step 11: String 1 black, 1 large bugle, 1 black, 1 blue, 1 black, 1 large bugle, and 1 black. Pass back through the blue at the middle of the next net.

Step 12: Rep Step 11 for the length of the collar.

Step 13: When you complete the last net for this row, string 1 black, 1 large bugle, 1 black, 1 blue, 1 black, 1 large bugle, 1 black, 1 blue, 1 black, 1 large bugle, 1 blue. Pass through the black in the middle of the last net on Row 1. Pass through beads so that you exit from the first blue strung in this step toward the bulk of the necklace.

Step 14: Work very loose. String 5 black. Pass through the black, blue, black middle of the next net.

Step 15: Rep Step 14 for the length of the collar.

Step 16: Weave through the beads in the upper netting rows so that you exit the first blue and the first black bead of the previous net in the opposite direction. Work the length of the collar in peyote stitch (3 beads total for each section).

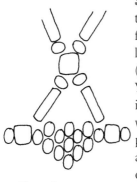

Figure 2

Step 17: Weave through the beads so that you turn the thread and exit from the last bead added. Work the length of the collar in peyote stitch (2 beads total for each section). You're making decreases, so for each individual section you'll need to weave your beads through the black peyote, up through the blue bead, and down through the black peyote of the next section to get to the spot where you add beads (Figure 2).

Step 18: Weave through the beads so that you turn the thread and exit from the last bead added. String 1 black and 1 blue. Pass through the black and the next-to-last bead added in Step 17. This will give you a picot. Rep this step for each section for the length of the collar. Exit from the side point of the peyote dart.

Step 19: String 13 black. Pass through the last blue strung. *String 12 black. Pass through the blue from the next section. Rep from * for the length of the collar. For the last net, string 13 and pass back through the bead at the side point of the last peyote dart. Weave your thread through the beads so that you exit the sixth bead just strung.

Step 20: *String 5 black, 1 blue, and 5 black. Pass through the middle two beads of the net in Step 19. Rep from * across the length of the collar. Exit from the sixth bead of the net from the previous row.

Step 21: Work loose. *String 13 black. Pass through the last blue strung in the previous net row. Rep from * across the length of the collar.

Step 22: Weave your thread through the beads so you are going in the opposite direction. Using black, work across the length of the collar in peyote stitch for 6 beads total in each section.

Step 23: Turn your thread through the beads so you are going in the opposite direction. Using black, work across the length of the collar in peyote stitch for a total of 5 beads each section, but instead of weaving up through the beads, just string 1 black between each section of peyote (under the blue of the previous row). Continue across the length of the collar.

Step 24: Turn your thread through the beads so you are going in the opposite direction. Using blue, work across the length of the collar in peyote stitch for 4 beads total in each section.

Step 25: Turn your thread through the beads so you are going in the opposite direction. Using blue, work across the length of the collar in peyote stitch for 3 beads in each section. Between sections string 1 black, 1 faceted, and 1 black (Figure 3).

Figure 3

Step 26: Add a clasp at the Victorian Chain level. Just sew it onto the blue beads that are at the edges. Be sure to make many stitches so that it is secure. It's best to use a clasp that has more than one anchor.

FRINGE

The collar shown has heavy-duty fringe. Not only does it feel nice, it weighs down the scalloped edges that can otherwise get a little too ruffled.

Begin with simple fringe (2 black, 1 large tube, 5 black in a picot and one leaf for each section) at the back until about ⅓ of the way around the necklace. Then start adding little bugles, one big bugle, and increase 1 black every fringe leg. Near the middle, add faceted beads for a subtle glimmer.

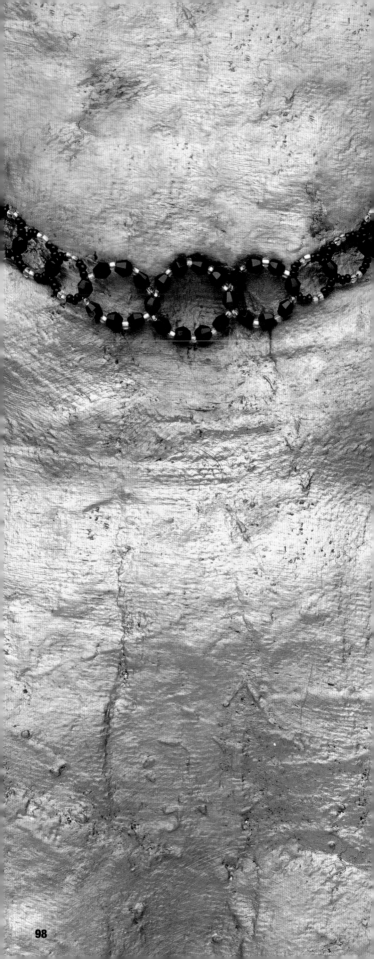

Beaded Tattoo

Suzanne Helwig

Materials
51 faceted 4mm black beads
Size 11° black seed beads
Size 11° gold seed beads
Approx. 24" of 20-gauge 14K gold-filled half-hard wire
Gold head pin
4½' of black Soft Flex .014" beading wire
2 gold-filled tubular crimp beads

Notions
Wire cutter
Crimping pliers
Round-nose pliers
WigJig Cyclops
Hammer and anvil
Cup bur

This choker is a very elegant version of the elastic tattoos made so popular by the younger set.

Step 1: Use the Soft Flex wire to string 3 black seed beads, 1 gold seed bead, 3 black seed beads, one crimp bead, 3 black seed beads, 1 gold seed bead, 3 black seed beads, and one 4mm. Center on the strand. Pass back through the last 4mm with one end of the wire, and snug up the beads to form Loop 1 (Figure 1).

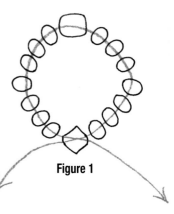

Figure 1

Step 2: String 3 black seed beads, 2 gold seed beads, and 3 black seed beads on each wire end. String one 4mm on one end of the wire, pass back through with the other end, and snug up the beads to form Loop 2. Repeat this step nine times to form Loops 3–11.

Step 3: String 1 gold seed bead, one 4mm, 1 gold seed bead, one 4mm, 1 gold seed bead, one 4mm, and 1 gold seed bead on each wire end. String one 4mm on one end of the wire and pass back through with the other end to form Loop 12.

Step 4: String 1 gold seed bead, one 4mm, 1 gold seed bead, one 4mm, 1 gold seed bead, one 4mm, 1 gold seed bead, one 4mm, and 1 gold seed bead on each wire end. String one 4mm on one end of the wire and pass back through with the other wire end to form Loop 13 (the center loop).

Step 5: Work the necklace in reverse order, starting with Step 3 and ending with Step 2.

Step 6: String 3 black seed beads, 1 gold seed bead, and 3 black seed beads on each wire end. String one crimp bead on one wire end and pass back through with the other end to form the last loop. Crimp the bead and cut the wire close to the work.

MAKING THE CHAIN

Step 7: String the gold wire though a 4mm bead. Make a loop. Snug the bead to the loop and measure about ½" from the bead on the other side of the wire; cut. Make another loop going in the opposite direction as the first loop. Make seven loops.

Step 8: Use the head pin to string 2 gold seed beads, one 4mm, 1 gold seed bead. Make a hangman's noose loop.

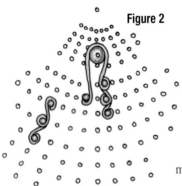

Figure 2

Step 9: Follow the jig pattern (Figure 2) to make eight chain links and a hook. File the end of the hook with a cup bur to smooth. For a professional finish, flatten and harden the wire components with a hammer and anvil.

Step 10: Assemble the chain by attaching a link to one end of the beaded portion of the necklace, then a bead/loop unit made in Step 10. Repeat three times. Finish with a hook.

Step 11: Repeat Step 13 for the other end of the necklace. Finish with the unit made in Step 11.

Suzanne Helwig is a jewelry designer for WigJig, the inventors of the original transparent wire jigs. Reach her through Wigjig's internet store for jigs, beads, jewelry supplies, tools, and books at www.wigjig.com.

Tubular Triangles Necklace

Jane Tyson

Materials

10 gr. size 11° seed beads
10 gr. size 11° Toho Triangles
6 x 6mm faceted round beads
Silamide beading thread in color to
      complement the beads
Gossamer Floss

Notions

Size 12 beading needle
Scissors

This pretty little necklace consists of a number of tubes made from alternating rows of triangles and seed beads worked in square stitch. When a row of triangles is completed, it looks like a pie cut into six wedges. Completing the assembly, the Gossamer Floss makes the necklace elastic enough to slip right over your head.

Step 1: Using a yard of thread and leaving an 8" tail, string 2 triangles. Make a ladder using six triangle beads and join them in a circle to make a pie. Be sure to work the triangles together firmly.

Step 2: String 2 seed beads and pass down through the second triangle. Pass up through the third triangle, string 1 seed bead, and pass down through the second seed bead and triangle. Pass up through the third triangle and seed bead, string 1 seed bead, and pass down through the fourth triangle. Pass up through the fifth triangle, string 1 seed bead, pass back down through the fourth seed bead and triangle, and pass back up through the fifth triangle and seed bead. String 1 seed bead, pass down through the sixth triangle and pass back up

through the first triangle and seed bead. You should have a thread joining each seed bead to the next one in your row (Figure 1).

Figure 1

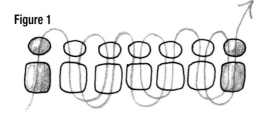

Step 3: Repeat Step 2 for 17 rows alternating triangles and seed beads. Finish with a row of triangles. Weave the tail and working threads into the beadwork to create a tight tube. Trim close to work. Make one tube and calculate the length of necklace you require before making more tubes.

Step 4: When you have completed your tubes, thread the wire needle over the end of the Gossamer Floss (do not cut from the card). Using about a yard of floss, pass through a tube. String a faceted bead, a tube, and then a faceted bead. Continue to alternate until all the tubes and beads are on the floss. Pass through the necklace a second time, making sure that the tail doesn't get pulled through. Stretch the necklace out until the floss sits evenly around the necklace and there is no excess. Tie a tight knot in the tail and needle end of the floss, close to the necklace. Don't be afraid to tie the knots tight. Trim the excess Gossamer Floss. Now you can curve each tube to make the necklace round.

Jane Tyson is a Tasmanian beadwork teacher and bead seller. She can be contacted at jrtyson@netspace.net.au.

Chain Link

Jean Campbell

Materials
80" of 20-gauge silver wire
4mm hematite beads
7mm freshwater pearls
6mm liquid silver beads

Notions
Wire cutter
Round-nose pliers

This is a very simple necklace that's suitable for work or weekend wear.

Step 1: Without cutting the silver wire, string 1 hematite, 1 pearl, and 1 hematite. Make a loop at the very end of the wire with your round-nose pliers. Push the beads down to the loop and cut the wire ⅜" from the last hematite. Make a loop at that end of the wire. Make 24.

Step 2: Repeat Step 1, but instead of hematite and pearls, string liquid silver beads. Make 24.

Step 3: Connect the lengths made in Steps 1 and 2, alternating as you go. Always open the loops laterally, never horizontally.

Tips

STARTING A NEW THREAD

There's no doubt that you'll run out of thread as you work on your necklaces that use off-loom stitches. It's easy to begin a new thread. There are a couple of solutions. I prefer the first way because it's stronger.

Solution 1: Tie off your old thread when it's about 4" long by making a simple knot between beads. Pass through a few beads and pull tight to hide the knot. Weave through a few more beads and trim the thread close to the work. Start the new thread by tying a knot between beads and weaving through a few beads. Pull tight to hide the knot. Weave through several beads until you reach the place to begin again.

Solution 2: Here's how to end your old thread without tying a knot. Weave the thread in and out, around and around, through several beads and then trim it close to the work. Begin a new thread the same way, weaving the end of the thread in and out, around and around, and through several beads until you reach the place to begin again.

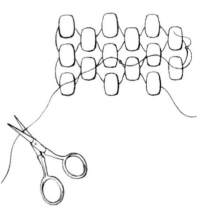

PASS THROUGH VS. PASS BACK THROUGH

Pass through means to move your needle in the same direction as the beads have been strung. Pass back through means to move your needle in the opposite direction.

TENSION BEAD

A tension bead holds your work in place. To make one, string a bead larger than those you are working with, then pass through the bead again, making sure not to split your thread. The bead will be able to slide along, but will still provide tension to work against.

$\mathcal{S}$titches

Ladder

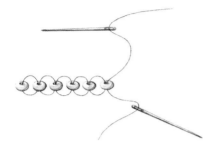

Using two needles, one threaded on each end of the thread, pass one needle through one or more beads from left to right and pass the other needle through the same beads from right to left. Continue adding beads by crisscrossing both needles through one bead at a time. Use this stitch to make strings of beads or as the foundation for brick stitch.

Netting

Begin by stringing a base row of 13 beads. String 5 beads and go back through the fifth bead from the end of the base row. String another 5 beads, skip 3 beads of the base row, and go back through the next. Rep to end of row. PT the fifth, fourth, and third beads of those just strung, exiting from the third. Turn the work over and go back across the same way.

Peyote

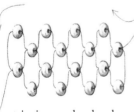

This stitch can also be referred to as gourd stitch.

One-drop peyote begins by stringing an even number of beads to create the first two rows. Begin the third row by stringing one bead and passing through the second-to-last bead of the previous rows. String another bead and pass through the fourth-to-last bead of the previous rows. Continue adding one bead at a time, passing over every other bead of the previous rows.

Two-drop peyote is worked the same as above, but with two beads at a time instead of one.

Two-needle right angle weave

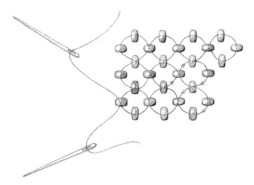

Using two needles, one on each end of the thread, string three beads and slide them to the center of the thread. Pick up a fourth bead, pass one needle through from left to right and pass the other needle through from right to left. Pick up one bead with each needle, then pick up one more bead and pass one needle through from left to right and pass the other needle through from right to left. Continue for desired length of row. To work next row, repeat as for first row, stringing new beads only onto the right thread and passing back through beads from first row with the left thread.

To make a row-end decrease, simply stop your row short and begin a new row.

Square

Begin by stringing a row of beads. For the second row, string 2 beads, pass through the second-to-last bead of the first row, and back through the second bead of those just strung. Continue by stringing 1 bead, passing through the

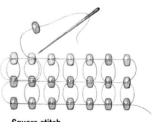

Square stitch

third-to-last bead of the first row, and back through the bead just strung. Repeat this looping technique across to the end of the row.

To make a decrease, weave thread through the previous row and exit from the bead adjacent to the place you want to decrease. Continue working in square stitch.

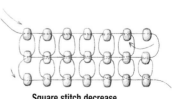

Square stitch decrease

Hangman's noose loop

Cut desired length of wire and make a 90°
bend 2" from one end. Make a ½" loop with
the bent end and coil the wire tightly down
the neck of the wire to finish. Use to link
beads or to finish a wire-worked piece.

Wire loop

Grasp one end of the wire with round-nose
pliers. Holding on to the wire with one hand,
gently turn the pliers until the wire end and
wire body touch. Create a 90° reverse bend
where they meet.

Herringbone

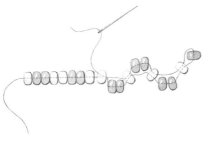

This weave is often
found in the bead-
work of the South
African Ndebele tribe.
For purposes of illus-
tration, we show
alternating rows of
two colors. You can,
of course, use one
color or any number.

String 16 beads as follows: 1 light, 2 dark, 2 light, 2 dark, 2
light, 2 dark, 2 light, 2 dark, 1 light. Leave a 6" tail.

Rows 1–3: String 1 dark bead. Pass back through the last light
bead strung. Skip 2 dark beads and pass through the next light
bead. String 2 dark beads. Pass through the next light bead.
Skip 2 dark beads. Pass through the next light bead. String 2
dark beads. Pass through the next light bead. Skip 2 dark
beads. Pass through the next light bead. String 2 dark beads.
Pass through the next light bead. Skip 2 dark beads. Pass
through the last light bead.

Row 4: String 1 dark and 1 light bead. Pass back through the
dark bead just strung. *Pass through the first bead of the next
2-bead set. String 2 light beads. Pass through the next dark
bead. Repeat from * until you've reached the end of the row.

Row 5: Turn work over. String 1 light bead and 1 dark bead.
Pass back through the light bead just strung. *Pass through the
first bead of the next 2-bead set. String 2 dark beads. Pass
through the next light bead. Repeat from * to end of row.
Continue working in alternating pattern to desired length.

Bead embroidery

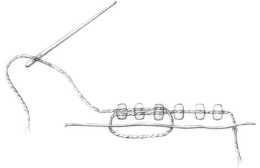

Begin by passing the needle through the fabric, from wrong side to right side. String 3 beads and pass back through the fabric to the left of where the third bead lies. Bring the needle back through the fabric to the right of the bead, pass back through the bead. You can sew up to three beads per stitch by stringing 3 beads and backstitching through the third as shown.

Bead crochet

As with bead knitting, traditional bead crochet is done with fine silk thread or pearl cotton and small seed beads. We do not explain how to crochet, only how to incorporate beads into your crochet work. Begin with beads strung onto thread as for knitting.

Bead crochet in rounds (a)

Bead crochet in rounds (b)

Bead crochet in rounds yields a very dense, continuous surface. To work a bead in single crochet, insert the hook into the back of the stitch, put the yarn over the hook and draw a loop through— you now have two loops on the hook. Slide a bead up to the loops, wrap yarn over the hook, and draw the yarn through the loops. The bead will be fixed to the back side of the crocheted work.

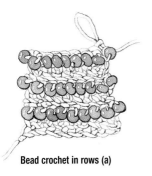

Bead crochet in rows (a)

Bead crochet in rows is worked back and forth, but beads can only be worked on alternate rows.

To form a continuous surface, you must work entirely from the same side, cutting the yarn at the end of each row.

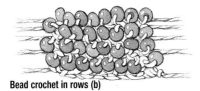

Bead crochet in rows (b)

Beaded crochet cord makes a great finish or a strap for other beadwork. Make an initial chain of four (or more) stitches, leaving a bead in each chain stitch by sliding a bead close to the hook before making each stitch. Form a ring of beaded stitches by inserting the hook into the first chain stitch, under the thread carrying the bead. Move the bead to the right of the hook.

Bead crochet cord (a)

Slide a new bead down close to the hook and work a slip stitch by pulling a loop of thread through both the loops on the hook. Make a slip stitch with a bead into each of the remaining chain stitches to complete the first round. Continue working beaded slip stitches in a spiral to the length desired.

Bead crochet cord (b)